DOING PRACTITIONER
RESEARCH

DOING PRACTITIONER
RESEARCH

MARK FOX, PETER MARTIN & GILL GREEN

SAGE Publications
London ▪ Los Angeles ▪ New Delhi ▪ Singapore

First published 2007

SAGE Publications Ltd
1 Oliver's Yard
55 City Road
London EC1Y 1SP

SAGE Publications Inc.
2455 Teller Road
Thousand Oaks, California 91320

SAGE Publications India Pvt Ltd
B 1/I 1 Mohan Cooperative Industrial Area
Mathura Road, New Delhi 110 044
India

SAGE Publications Asia-Pacific Pte Ltd
33 Pekin Street #02-01
Far East Square
Singapore 048763

British Library Cataloguing in Publication data

A catalogue record for this book is available from the British Library

ISBN 978 1 4129 1233 4
ISBN 978 1 4129 1234 1(pbk)

Library of Congress Control Number: 2006929060

Typeset by C&M Digitals (P) Ltd, Chennai, India
Printed in Great Britain by The Cromwell Press Ltd, Trowbridge, Wiltshire
Printed on paper from sustainable resources

Contents

Introduction

This book is written for practitioners working in health, education and social care who are undertaking research. Practitioner research is an emerging research tradition. The aim of practitioner research is fundamentally no different from other forms of research in that it is about generating new knowledge. Nor are there unique research techniques attached to it. However, practitioner researchers *are* different as a result of their unique position in the research process. It is this uniqueness that we wish to capture in this book by focusing on its particular strengths, as well as its weaknesses. This book attempts to highlight the very real issues that practitioners face when undertaking research. By doing so it attempts to show the value of practitioner research and how it is critical to the effective development of practitioners.

The Practitioner Researcher

This book is for practitioners engaged in research primarily in the public sector. The words 'practitioner' and 'professional' are used interchangeably in this book. A practitioner researcher is someone who is employed in a professional capacity but who, as part of their role, is expected to undertake research. With the present emphasis on accountability, evidence-based practice and evaluation, practitioners are increasingly becoming engaged in some kind of research. This research may be about keeping detailed records of a child's progress, evaluating how a service is performing or ensuring service users' views are taken into account when planning developments in services. Such research may be carried out as a specific aspect of the practitioner's role, it may be an additional seconded role for a fixed period or it may be quite hidden from view. The research may be part of a higher or further degree or it may be independent of any academic qualification.

Being a practitioner researcher is not the same as being an academic researcher. The practitioner researcher approaches research and embeds research within practice in ways that an academic researcher cannot.

Fundamentally, we believe that there is a synergy between research and practice for the practitioner researcher in that practitioners engaged in research are more successful practitioners and researchers engaged in practice are more successful researchers.

Yet, the practitioner researchers with whom we work have implicitly and explicitly indicated that their research is seen as less important than that of academic researchers. It is our intention to redress this imbalance and legitimise people's research into their own practice.

For example, occupational therapists have a unique and distinct perspective of the world. Research that seeks to understand and develop the practice of occupational therapy cannot be controlled and directed by a medical doctor or an academic sociologist. This is not to dismiss the contribution of academics from different disciplines. It can offer a different perspective on an issue that opens up, for the practitioners, new ways of developing their practice. However, in this book we want to identify the unique contribution of practitioner researchers.

On Being a Practitioner in the Public Sector

In the UK, the state both directly, through the government, or indirectly, through local and regional structures such as local authorities and Primary Care Trusts, runs a range of services and agencies. These include the National Health Service (the largest employer in the world) and local authorities, which includes schools and social services. In addition, the state supports directly or indirectly a range of other non-statutory organisations that also employ professionals.

A very wide variety of professionals work in these large public sector institutions. Professional groups usually share a similar perspective, inculcated throughout training, and the culture of their professional associations. However, professionals often have quite radical differences on the underpinning basis of delivering services to patients, clients or pupils.

One of the key aspects of the government's agenda is to ensure that public services work more effectively. This requires a greater degree of 'joined up' thinking throughout the organisations. This drive is both at the micro level for professionals within services to work more effectively together, and also at a macro level for services as organisations to work together.

Difficulties with joined up thinking within research arise at a number of levels. Most fundamentally they arise because different professional groups work from different research bases, promoting different research methodologies and types of knowledge. Research across the different professions is not joined up and, therefore, research across different agencies is often never connected. In addition, academic researchers working in different disciplines are encouraged to target their research for particular academic audiences. Practitioner research usually has a focus on the real problems that individuals face. Practitioner researchers have the opportunity to promote research that is joined up and break the academic, fragmented approach to knowledge.

Evidence-Based Practice

Over the past few years the government has affirmed that there must be a clear link between professional practice and research. This is known as evidence-based practice. The development of evidence-based practice has three components. The first, and most important, is that research should provide the evidence on which professional practice is based. The second component is that service delivery will change based on best available research evidence. The third component is that, through evaluation of services, practitioners can monitor the effects of their interventions.

In response to the development of an evidence-based practice culture, practitioners are encouraged, and sometimes coerced, to engage more actively with research. An increasing number of practitioners have a research remit as it is widely recognised that the connection between professional practice and research is best achieved through the development of practitioner research whereby practitioners undertake research into their own practice. If this is to happen, practitioners need to develop the skills and also the authority to research their own practice. This book supports practitioner researchers to fulfil this role.

Our Position

We work at the University of Essex in the Department of Health and Human Sciences. This is a multi-professional and multi-disciplinary department and we have tried to capture the multi-professional ethos within this text. In writing the text our backgrounds in education, psychology, sociology and nursing kept intervening in our discussions. At first this was an irritation that interrupted the free flow of discussion, but as we progressed we recognised that this represented the 'real world' problems that practitioner researchers face and began to incorporate this debate into our writing.

We have included many examples of practitioner research drawn from our own practice. Whilst we have removed the personal and identifiable details from the examples, each case study represents real debates in which we have engaged with practitioners, students and each other. These case studies highlight the range of issues that face practitioner researchers and illustrate how practitioner research is still at a developmental stage without pre-formed answers to many of the issues. This book draws together our current understanding as a precursor to further development in the future.

When we first discussed writing this book we were concerned at the apparent absence of joined up thinking within the public services. We decided that the book would attempt to draw out common themes in health care, social care and education. Many of our colleagues argued that it could not be done. Academic and professional colleagues felt that there was too much difference between the health, education and social care sectors. What we have found in our discussion whilst writing the book is that there is actually a great deal of overlap. The basis of the problems that tax teachers are often also experienced by health and social care staff.

We believe that the practitioner researcher has a significant role to play in the development of our public services. This role is in its infancy at present and this book offers a glimpse at the terrain as it is currently mapped. We find it very exciting that this landscape has very few features drawn onto it. This is a map only in the sense that it provides us with an indication of where the landscape starts and finishes.

This is not a do-it-yourself textbook. The world in which the practitioner researcher operates is so varied that such a book would be too generic and, consequently, of very limited use. What we have tried to do is write a book that encapsulates some of the debates that currently surround practitioner research. We do not offer answers, but instead, the opportunity to engage with the debate, reflect on your own practice and form your own opinions.

Structure of the Book

There are 11 chapters that address different substantive issues. Each chapter includes case studies drawn from our own experience to illustrate the impact of the theoretical content upon the practitioner researcher in the real world.

Chapter 1 examines the different research worlds in which practitioner researchers operate and links these with the range of research paradigms used by practitioner researchers. It asks what constitutes good quality research and assesses the potential for combining different research methods in practitioner research.

Chapter 2 explores how the practitioner researcher's personal and professional background impacts upon the research agenda. It examines different types of knowledge – propositional, process, personal and value-based knowledge. It encourages practitioner researchers to reflect upon and think critically about their practice and the practice environment in relation to their research ideas. Such critical thinking assists practitioner researchers to define relevant theory, and examine the assumptions underpinning practice, within the framework of their research.

Chapter 3 makes the connection between research and development within organisations. Types of research that support and facilitate development are explored at both an individual (micro) and organisational (macro) level.

Chapter 4 examines the unique position of the practitioner researcher in terms of conducting evaluative research within their own organisation. It explores the advantages that the practitioner researcher has, particularly their access to the 'shadow side' of organisations. Different types of evaluation frameworks used in both process and outcome research are examined.

Chapter 5 looks at the strengths and weaknesses of practitioner researchers carrying out research within their own practice. Whilst the practitioner researcher can engage in strategies to clarify roles within the research process, the boundaries between 'practitioner as practitioner' and 'practitioner as researcher' tend to be blurred and unfixed. This chapter links practitioner research to professional development and identifies research as an opportunity for practice development.

Chapter 6 looks at the concept of doing ethical research and takes a critical stance towards the burgeoning national structures that have been established in the past decade to control research within public services. It argues that there is a need for systems to ensure that all research meets appropriate ethical standards and provides some helpful strategies to support practitioner researchers through the bureaucracy.

Chapter 7 provides an overview of the research process focusing particularly on getting the research proposal right. It identifies a range of practical issues encountered during the research journey and stresses the need for careful planning at all stages. Strategies to assist with research planning are suggested.

Chapter 8 examines the role service users have to play within practitioner research and how this role can be facilitated. Establishing collaboration with service users is challenging and it can be difficult to avoid involvement that is tokenistic. This chapter focuses on styles of involvement and how to establish effective engagement with service users as collaborative partners. Issues relating to ownership of research conducted in collaboration with service users are discussed.

Chapter 9 is concerned with how practitioner researchers present their research and looks at writing the research report. It suggests strategies to assist writing, such as keeping a research diary to ensure that writing up is an on-going process throughout the research. It also encourages the practitioner researcher to reflect upon the target audience to identify the most appropriate form of dissemination of the research results.

Chapter 10 examines how practitioner researchers can maximise the impact of their research. Incorporating research findings into practice within organisations is complex, but it is equally challenging for individual practitioners to change safe and familiar practice. The advantages of working collaboratively are explored in order to promote joined up thinking.

Chapter 11 explores how we can facilitate the growth and development of practitioner researchers. The importance of reflection leading to reflexivity is explored as is the use of supervision to aid development. Techniques for developing reflective skills are discussed as an aid to developing the practitioner researcher.

The final chapter collates our conclusions about practitioner research based on our experience of researching and writing the chapters. It highlights the uniqueness of practitioner research for personal development and its potential to change practice.

We have not identified the real names of people within our case studies, but we do want to acknowledge the significant contribution of all those individuals both to our thinking and to the finished product. The case studies acted as the trigger for writing the book and served to crystallise our thinking about who we were writing for. We have addressed the problems brought to us by practitioners through our own reflection on research and practice and by talking to one another. In that respect the book is a dialogue of the sort of discussions that have taken place in the Department of Health and Human Sciences in the past few years. If we have captured some of the immediacy of that debate then we have achieved our aim.

1
Framing Research

Practitioner researchers use a range of research paradigms as a basis for practice. Underpinning these research paradigms are different ways of looking at what is 'real'. These lead to different ways of researching reality and defining what is good research. Practitioner researchers need to integrate the strengths, and acknowledge the weaknesses, of different research paradigms, especially when working in a collaborative way with colleagues from different disciplines. In particular, the chapter deals with:

⇨ Identifying areas to research
⇨ Research worlds
⇨ Different research paradigms
⇨ Good quality research
⇨ Combining different research methods

1.1 IDENTIFYING AREAS TO RESEARCH

The starting point for practitioner researchers is to formulate an answerable question for a service issue. This seems quite simple but actually it highlights some of the fundamental complexities of undertaking research.

Case Study:
Sam – clarifying the issues

Sam has been referred to a practitioner in a local service. She is an adolescent girl. She spends most of her time in her bedroom at home watching the TV. She will speak to her parents only under great duress from them. She is very thin.

Different practitioners will have different ideas about Sam and whether she has a problem or not. What are your immediate responses to Sam?

Different practitioners will focus on different aspects of the situation and have different suggestions about how Sam can be helped.

- Some practitioners may think she is depressed. They may want to treat her with drugs, or talking therapy, or working with her family
- Some practitioners may think she is socially isolated and want her to stop watching TV and to go out more and make friends
- Some practitioners may think that she is on drugs. They may want to treat her by getting her off the drugs and stop her spending time with her friends
- Some practitioners may think that it is a developmental stage she is going through. They want the other professionals not to worry and leave her alone

How practitioners react and the hypothesis that they come up with will at least partially depend on their professional background, training and experience. It will also depend on which service they work for – her school, children's services, the primary care trust or a voluntary organisation. The organisation they work for will also have views on what an appropriate response should be.

Gathering Information

The next stage for many practitioners is to gain more knowledge about Sam by gathering more information. In this way they are researching the problem. The information gathered depends upon the initial hypotheses. The focus here is not on *how* information is gathered but on *what* is gathered.

For some practitioners gathering more objective facts about Sam is important. Facts can be: how old she is; what school she attends; what she weighs; are there traces of drugs in her body; how many brothers and sisters she has; what is her reading age? These are objective facts.

There are other aspects of Sam's life that it may be important to find out about but that are not considered facts. We may want to know how she relates to her sisters or how many friends she has. But the answer to this depends on how 'a friend' is defined. We may want to know more about her self-esteem. These things are socially constructed. Much of the information that practitioners work with is socially constructed.

There is a further type of information. Sam may have a view of friends that is different from what the practitioner means by 'friendship'. The practitioner may define it in a way that she does not accept. Sam may consider everyone in her class that talks to her as a friend whereas the practitioner may have a different definition.

Different types of information are required to begin to understand Sam. The types of knowledge are based on different understandings of 'reality' and for each reality there are different ways of researching it.

1.2   RESEARCH WORLDS

One of the fundamental questions in philosophy is about the nature of the world. This is known as ontology or the nature of reality. Some practitioners' disciplines are closely allied to one particular view. For example, most medical practitioners are closely allied to an objective world-view. On the other hand, social workers are allied to the idea of a socially constructed world. Some disciplines seem to move between the various models.

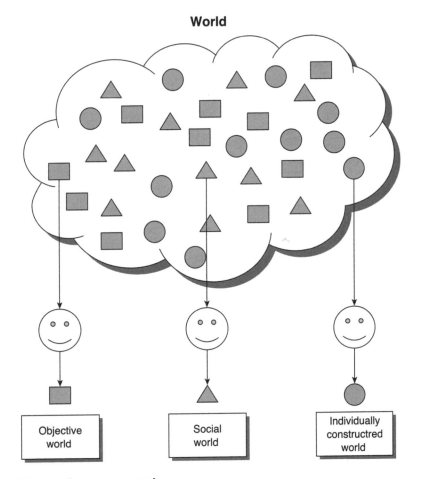

FIGURE 1.1   *Areas to research*

The Objective World

Realists take the view that there is a real objective 'world which exists independent of human belief, perception, culture and language we use to describe it' (Hart, 1998: 85). This world is observable and research can be used to verify, using reliable measures, the existence of something. This thinking developed from the nineteenth-century philosophical position known as positivism that later became known as logical positivism (Popper, 1959). The term 'positivism' originally meant progressive in the belief that knowledge needed to be value-free and not affected by the philosophical or cultural beliefs of the day.

The Socially Constructed World

Another research world is the shared meanings about the world constructed by groups of people. In this area there is not one objective or true reality but a shared social reality constructed through language. Reality is socially constructed by different groups of people or cultures. There are multiple realities and groups construct a reality to make sense of their world. The classic example of this is Benjamin Lee Whorf's description of how Eskimos have 45 different words for snow (Whorf, 1956). He argues that because they have 45 different words for snow they see 45 different kinds of snow. The focus of the research is on how groups of people use language to construct a social reality.

   In the same way professions develop their own elaborated language, which gives them a distinct view of the world that may be different from that of a person outside this profession. The language people use and how they construct the world is connected to a particular point in time and social perspective. So the way that medical practitioners construct depression is located within a particular time (early twenty-first century) and place (Britain, or at least the Western world). This would be very different from the understanding of depression in different centuries or in different areas of the world. Therefore Sam's behaviour is given meaning by particular practitioners within a particular context.

The Individually Constructed World

The final research world is how an individual constructs or experiences his or her own reality (Watzlawick, 1978). This area for research is interested in how even within a small community, for example a family, there is no shared construction and understanding of a past event. Instead, each individual holds a unique story about what has happened in the past – an aspect of life brilliantly exposed by the plays of Harold Pinter. This stems from a phenomenological approach that accepts there is nothing more fundamental than experiences (see Smith, 2003 for a fuller explanation). Reality is what a person experiences and this is what should be researched. Phenomenology celebrates what is unique about an individual. The importance of understanding the individual construction of the world is supported by cognitive biologists who have shown that there is not a straightforward correspondence between an external stimulus and the reactions of the senses. Instead, it appears that each individual selects how they are going to respond to the same stimulus (Maturana and Varela, 1980). Phenomenologists believe that reality is how the individual makes sense of and constructs his or her own world.

So there are different types of reality to understand about Sam. Each of these areas – objective, socially constructed and individually constructed – can be researched in terms of a systematic investigation leading to an increase in knowledge. The type of reality that the practitioner researcher is interested in leads to different types of research.

1.3   DIFFERENT RESEARCH PARADIGMS

Researching the Objective World

Practitioners who are interested in researching the objective world use what is traditionally known as scientific research. Scientific research is characterised by experiments where data are gathered that critically test hypotheses. Scientific research attempts to systematise knowledge through generalisable principles. The data that are collected are usually in the form of numbers. This type of research is often referred to as quantitative research because the focus is upon quantities in relation to the subject of study.

Quantitative research traditionally takes a positivist approach. Positivism has its roots in research in the natural sciences – physics, chemistry and biology – and is seen to be objective. It takes the position that scientific knowledge is a direct reflection of a real and objective world. In recent years, post-positivism has replaced positivism as the most appropriate thinking about quantitative research (see Clark, 1998). Post-positivism continues to take the view that there is a reality that research should investigate. However, it proposes that this truth can only be slowly and imperfectly arrived at given the limitations of the research process. It also accepts that the researcher cannot take a neutral or value-free position in the research. The researcher's background helps shape the research and its results. The aim is still to be objective but there is a recognition that this is impossible.

The way the real, objective world can be understood is through experimental (or hypothetical-deductive) research. The purest form of scientific research is the experiment. An experiment has four key features:

- The random assignment of participants to either an experimental group or a 'no treatment' control group
- Intervention by changing one or more variables (called 'independent variables') by the researcher
- The measurement of the effects of this change on one or more other variables (called 'dependent variables') through using pre-and post-test measures
- The control of all other variables

(adapted from Robson, 2002: 110)

True experiments involve the random assignment of participants to different conditions. Sometimes it is not possible to meet all these conditions so a variety of quasi-experimental designs can be used.

- If it is not possible to assign participants randomly to two groups the groups can be established on some other basis – for example, by matching
- If it is not possible to have two groups then a series of measures over time can be taken on the one set of subjects who are subject to some kind of intervention – this is known as impact or policy analysis
- If it is possible to have only a single participant this is a type of quasi-experiment called a single case design

In all these examples the purpose is to find out something that is true for other people in similar circumstances or generalisable. As well as experiments there are other ways of researching the objective world through gathering quantitative data. A survey using a fixed response (tick box) format can be used to generate knowledge. This type of objective knowledge is seen to be applicable to the whole population. That is why the participants in this type of survey are so carefully sampled. They have to represent everybody in the target population.

These types of positivist research are designed to find out truth in a real objective world. The key features of this type of research are summarised in Box 1.1.

Box 1.1   Key features of researching the objective world

- The process of research is usually deductive
- Research is based on what can be measured
- The research process is fixed at the start of the research in terms of the number of participants and the measures being used
- A hypothesis is formulated based on previous research
- The hypothetical-deductive method involves testing hypotheses through an experiment

(Continued)

> (*Continued*)
> - Predictable relationships (cause/effect) between objects and events are sought
> - Reliable quantitative data are collected
> - Data are collected from a representative sample of people
> - Findings can be generalised
> - The researcher aims to be objective and neutral
> - Data are used to support or reject previous theory
>
> (see Hart, 1998: 83)

Scientific research holds out the possibility of generating knowledge that is more valid and reliable than personal opinion, fantasy or superstition.

Researching the Socially Constructed World

Researching the socially constructed world has many of the elements of the scientific approach. Knowledge is usually obtained from observation and open interviews rather than experiments. The data are critically analysed, and organised in a systematic way. The data are usually words and so this type of research is often referred to as *qualitative research*.

Tesch (1990) identified 26 different types of qualitative research. A few of these are central to the work of practitioner researchers and illustrate the main principles of research on socially constructed knowledge (see also Creswell, 2003).

Discourse analysis   Discourse analysis looks at texts to explore the functions served by specific constructions at both the interpersonal and societal level. Texts are all forms of verbal and written accounts, such as books, articles, newspapers and websites. They can be conversations and interactions in a classroom, ward or between members of a family. They can also be reports, case notes or a teacher's lesson plan. The researcher is interested in the way an account is linguistically constructed in terms of the descriptive, referential and rhetorical language that is used, and the function that it serves. Discourse analysis can aid understanding of how people construct texts to justify their position. Sometimes the interest is in simply understanding how the text has been constructed. However, more often discourse analysis is used to deconstruct a process. Discourse analysis has also been used extensively to identify ideologies, for example how racism or sexism is produced by the language people use.

Grounded theory The purpose of grounded theory is to develop new theoretical perspectives based on (or grounded in) people's actual experiences. It was first developed by sociologists Glaser and Strauss (1967) as a positivist research paradigm. However, it is now largely seen as a way of researching the socially constructed world. It is based on the idea that instead of obtaining information either to prove or disprove a previous theory, the researcher can develop new theoretical perspectives from studying what people actually say and do in relation to particular experiences. The research develops incrementally in so far that after the first interview is completed data is analysed. On the basis of this analysis more data is gathered either to support or refute the original analysis. The researcher tries to listen with an open mind – rather than starting with preconceptions about the area under investigation. Theory is generated as data are collected and frameworks are then developed and modified. The 'flip-flop' between ideas and research experience is central to the research and is fully recorded.

Ethnography   Ethnography has a long tradition in anthropology and sociology. It is designed to analyse organisations, cultures or communities in their natural settings. These communities are usually observed comprehensively and in depth over time. The researcher tries to make sense of how these systems organise and operate. For example, ethnographic research might examine what goes on in a hospital ward that leads to feelings of empowerment? Or what support does a visually impaired child get in school?

These are just three of the principal strategies of qualitative research designed to understand the social construction of the world. They are in themselves quite different to each other. However, they do share some common features (see Box 1.2).

Box 1.2   Key features of researching the socially constructed world

- The process of research is usually inductive
- Research is based on what can be made meaningful
- The research process is flexible in terms of the number of participants or the lengths of the interviews or observations
- It starts with a social phenomenon that the practitioner researcher wants to understand more about
- It is designed to find out how a group of people make sense of the world
- Rich qualitative data are collected
- Data are collected from a meaningful sample of people

(Continued)

(*Continued*)

- Research illuminates particular situations – generalisation is not normally possible
- The practitioner researcher recognises his/her own position in the research
- Data are interpreted by the researcher

Researching the Individually Constructed World

The final area that practitioner researchers are interested in is how an individual constructs his or her own world (see Schandt, 1994). The focus this time is on the individual's experience – a phenomenological approach. This can be contrasted with socially constructed research, where the focus is on how language (or other events) is used to construct a discourse or shared meaning between people. One of the major issues in phenomenological research is whether self-knowledge acquired through self-reflection or introspection is a valid form of knowledge. This has led to scepticism from positivist researchers.

This process is compounded by the fact that it is not simply one person engaged in this process – there is a participant and a practitioner researcher. It is not the participant alone who constructs his or her own reality but also the practitioner researcher who is part of that co-construction. The practitioner researcher's own language becomes central to the process of research. Practitioner researchers need to be aware how they construct the world. This becomes a key aspect of the research, known as reflexivity (see Chapter 11).

The involvement of the practitioner researcher in the research leads to two radically different positions (see Smith, 2003 for further details).

- Faithful disclosure: the researcher tries to convey the 'real' life view or meaning for individuals, such as what it is like for a person to have a degenerative condition
- Reframing: the researcher takes a 'suspicious' approach and tries to discover what is behind the individual's experience, such as aiming to discover what the person with a degenerative condition is trying to convey by telling us about their experiences

There are a range of research methods for understanding how individuals construct their worlds. Two particularly popular ones are interpretative phenomenological analysis and narrative research.

Interpretative phenomenological analysis (IPA) The researcher is interested in the subjective experiences of the participant (Smith, 2003). The research is designed to investigate an individuals' perception and the meaning they give to a phenomenon. Examples of IPA are 'What is it like to work on an acute psychiatric ward?', 'What is it like to be blind in a mainstream school?' The research procedure usually involves getting to know a small number of people in depth.

Narrative research   The researcher explores the lives of individuals and the story of their lives. Narratives are seen as the stories that individuals tell about themselves to give order to their lives. Data for narrative research are normally collected through interviews. The narrative interview is designed to allow the participant to give a detailed story about their life or part of it. Other forms of narrative research include the keeping of a journal or using photographs.

Phenomenological and socially constructed research share many of the same features (see Guba and Lincoln, 1994). Phenomenological research is always qualitative (see Box 1.3).

Box 1.3   Key features of researching the individually constructed world

- The process of research is largely inductive
- The focus is on how people make sense of their experiences
- There is recognition that other people may make similar sense of their experiences but that each account is unique
- The research starts with a personal phenomenon which the practitioner researcher wants to understand more about
- Rich qualitative data are collected
- Data are collected from a limited number of people
- The researcher recognises that he or she co-constructs the research
- Data are made sense of by the researcher through reflexivity
- Findings are constructions that are not more or less 'true' but more informed and sophisticated than previous constructions

---

The interest for practitioner researchers in individually constructed knowledge is that it is close to professional practice. Understanding the phenomenological experiences of individuals connects the practitioner to the practitioner researcher.

These three research worlds have been described as three distinct areas. There are, however, some grey areas between them. No knowledge is completely individually constructed. Usually there is some shared meaning between people and therefore in this way it is socially constructed. Similarly, there are socially constructed areas that may be researched as objective knowledge.

For example, there are socially defined conventions for describing the reading age of children or the anxiety levels of mental health patients. Instruments have been devised to measure individuals reading skills or levels of anxiety. In one way these areas are socially constructed. However, there comes a point where the social construction is so universally accepted that it is researched as objective truth.

1.4 THE QUALITY OF RESEARCH

Research in the objective world usually involves quantitative research, whereas research in the socially or individually constructed world usually involves qualitative research. The two traditions of quantitative and qualitative research have different beliefs about how the quality of research should be assessed.

Evaluating Quantitative Research

There are three main characteristics of good quantitative research: reliability, validity and generalisability. These three constructs underpin the main goal of quantitative research – replicability. Replicability is the idea that an independent researcher would obtain the same results by replicating the research.

A number of authors have written extensively on these three characteristics (see Robson, 2002 for a full discussion). They can be put into a series of questions that the practitioner researcher can ask about a piece of quantitative research to ascertain its value.

 Select a quantitative piece of research in your own area of work and critically evaluate it using the questions below to decide how good it is.

Reliability
- **Participant error and bias:** Are the participants or the circumstances in which the data were collected skewed or distorted?
- **Researcher error and bias:** Is the researcher objective and free from bias?

Validity
- **Construct validity:** Does the research technique actually measure what it claims to measure?
- **Internal validity:** Does the research plausibly demonstrate the causal relationship between the intervention and the outcome?

(Continued)

(*Continued*)

Generalisability (also known as external validity)
- ☑ **Generalisability:** Are the results of the research generalisable to populations in other settings?

Evaluating Qualitative Research

There is an on-going debate in qualitative research about how the evaluative concepts as applied in quantitative research (reliability, validity and generalisability) make any sense (see Morse et al., 2002). The concept of 'trustworthiness' was introduced by Guba and Lincoln (1981) as a way of broadening the debate. The value of qualitative research can be thought about both in terms of trustworthiness and in terms of validity and generalisation. Our framework follows the work and the writing of Elliott et al., 1999; Maxwell, 1992; Morse et al., 2002 and Stiles, 1999.

 Select a qualitative piece of research in your own area of work and critically evaluate it using the questions below to decide how good it is.

Validity
- ☑ **Descriptive validity:** Has the data been accurately collected for analysis?
- ☑ **Interpretative validity:** Is data distorted by the researcher's pre-set framework rather than emerging from the analysis?
- ☑ **Theory validity:** Are the data explained by appropriate theory?

Generalisability
- ☑ **Internal generalisability:** Are data distorted through selection of participants?
- ☑ **External validity:** Are the results generalisable?

In addition, qualitative research often looks for validity in terms of impact (see Stiles, 1999).

   The frameworks described above are used to highlight the sorts of issues that are of concern to quantitative and qualitative researchers to show that their research is trustworthy or valid. Practitioner researchers need to address these issues for their research to be seen as valuable.

1.5   HIERARCHY OF RESEARCH EVIDENCE

Health services research is dominated by a biomedical model based on an objective world-view of research. There is a belief that there are universalities to the treatment of illness. Research that is essentially scientific and quantitative is seen as providing the best quality. Within the NHS the standard for research is often seen as a hierarchy (see Box 1.4).

Box 1.4   Hierarchy of evidence for research in the objective world

- A systematic review of randomised controlled trials
- At least one randomised controlled trial
- At least one controlled study without randomisation
- At least one other type of quasi-experimental study
- Non-experimental descriptive study, such as comparative study, correlational studies, case controlled studies
- Qualitative studies
- Evidence from expert committee reports or opinions and/or clinical experience of respected authorities
- Individual opinion

The top of the hierachy – the 'gold standard' – for NHS research is a systematic review of randomised controlled trials (RCTs). These are published by the Cochrane Library, part of an international non-profit and independent organisation, dedicated to making up-to-date, accurate information about the effects of health care readily available worldwide. Systematic reviews are reviews of the research in an area. They can be helpfully seen as scientific investigations in themselves. The subject of the research is previously published research in a particular area and these papers are researched using a planned strategy. This strategy includes identifying all the relevant articles using clearly articulated criteria, analysis of the quality of the research design and then a synthesis of the findings from the different pieces of research.

If the quantitative results of the research are statistically combined it is known as a meta-analysis. If the results are summarised but not statistically combined it is known as a qualitative systematic review. Summaries of research that lack explicit descriptions of systematic methods are often called narrative or literature reviews.

An experimental design with randomised control of the participants is seen as the next best research. It can be seen that qualitative research, professional experience and individual opinion are at the bottom of the research hierarchy.

There is much debate within the research world about whether this hierarchy applies to all research or just to that pertaining to the objective world (see for example, Barnes et al., 1999). The argument in favour of RCTs is that they provide evidence about whether an intervention works. Within the NHS, NICE (National Institute for Clinical Excellence) recommends changes in professional practice based on evidence from this research hierarchy.

Other government organisations take a very different perspective on research. Within education there continues to be ambiguity about what constitutes quality research. The Department of Education and Employment's (DfEE's) review *Excellence in Research on Schools* explicitly states: 'We found no single objective definition of what actually constitutes "good quality" research' (DfEE, 1998: 2).

In social services there is a recognition that while other types of research are particularly important there is also a belief that RCTs may protect children from many of the changes in policy and practice that professionals inflict upon them (Sackett and Wenneberg, 1997).

The main problem with the use of RCTs, in the fields of social work and education, is that they 'tend to yield equivocal results' (Robson, 2002). Robson's summary of programmes that have been evaluated using RCT concludes that they do not consistently come up with clear findings – either positive or negative. This includes research in the fields of education and social work as well as criminology. In other words, the use of RCTs in medicine to produce clear results about the benefits of an intervention (usually chemical) has not been reproduced in other fields. Robson (2002) gives three explanations for this.

- **Interventions are ineffective**: This explanation suggests that the introduction of a particular programme or procedure is too 'weak' to have an effect
- **The design of the RCT is ineffective**: This explanation suggests that the problem is in how the research was carried out. For example, the sample may have been too small to see an effect or there may not have been genuine randomisation
- **RCTs are inappropriate**: This explanation suggests that the characteristics of people have a substantial impact on how they react to a programme or procedure. For example, different children respond differently to different reading programmes. Therefore by randomly allocating children to different

groups you are automatically washing out the major variable that affects the programme's effectiveness: that is, people's characteristics. This last explanation is also put forward by researchers using realist evaluation (see Chapter 4)

We have highlighted the difficulties of RCTs as it is important to recognise that they can become something of a holy grail. They may, however, be inappropriate and a hindrance for some practitioner researchers. The position this book takes is to recognise that research has different purposes that are best served by different research designs. The most common purposes of research are:

- Exploratory: understanding a little-known/researched phenomenon
- Descriptive: accurately portraying persons, events, situations
- Explanatory: explaining the relationship between or within phenomena
- Action: creating opportunities for change and empowerment
- Evaluative: establishing the worth of something

(see Robson, 2002 for further details)

1.6 MIXED METHODS FOR THE PRACTITIONER RESEARCHER

Combining the Quantitative and Qualitative Approach

Not only are there different purposes to research but also practitioners are faced with questions that require multifaceted answers. A mixed methods approach that uses qualitative and quantitative research can be helpful to many practitioner researchers (see Creswell, 2003). Different sorts of research can complement each other.

The central problem of combining qualitative and quantitative methods is that philosophically there are conflicts between the two paradigms. There are different assumptions about the nature of knowledge and how to obtain knowledge through research. However, these different paradigms can be combined as long as the practitioner researcher has a clear understanding of what the different paradigms will accomplish.

Take the example of Sam – our isolated teenager introduced earlier in this chapter. To help Sam, some objective knowledge is required. Equally, however, some knowledge about how she and her family and friends construct her difficulties and her own perception of them may be important.

Initially, quantitative and qualitative methods were combined as a way to cross-validate or 'triangulate' results on the same research question by using multiple methods (see, for example, Campbell and Stanley, 1963). There was an acknowledgement that all research methods have limitations and that convergence of results across different methods helps to validate findings.

Increasingly, however, combining qualitative and quantitative research is seen as a complementary process (Morgan, 1998). The key goal is to use the strength of one method to enhance the impact of the other. So information gained from one part of the study (either quantitative or qualitative) is used to strengthen the other aspect of the research. This is important to practitioner researchers who are often working on complex, multifaceted issues.

Research Designs based on Complementary Designs

The core of the complementary design is to use a qualitative and quantitative method for different, but well coordinated purposes within the same overall research project (see Morgan, 1998 for further details).

Two decisions are required:

- The priority decision
- The sequence decision

The priority decision   The first research decision determines which will be the principal tool for gathering the research data, whether the qualitative or quantitative method, and which will be the complementary method. The principal data collection method must have the strengths that are most important to the research purpose. The contrasting complementary method is one that can add further data to meet the principal purpose.

The sequence decision   The second research decision is the sequence or order in which the qualitative and quantitative methods are used. The sequence decision is based on the most effective way to optimise the effectiveness of the principal method. So the question is whether a preliminary input by the complementary method adds to the principal method or whether the complementary method is used as a follow-up to maximise the value of the principal method.

Box 1.5	Priority/sequence model for combining qualitative and quantitative research		
		Priority decision	
		Principal method: Quantitative	Principal method: Qualitative
Sequence decision	Complementary method: Preliminary	Smaller qualitative study helps guide the data collection in principally QUANTITATIVE study	Smaller quantitative study helps guide the data collection in a principallly QUALITATIVE study
		Example: Open-ended interviews with Sam and peers about the onset of depression is used to help devise an area-wide health survey for primary school children at risk of mental health problems	Example: A brief survey of self-esteem with adolescent girls in one school is used to identify girls to take part in a series of in-depth interviews
	Complementary method: Follow-up	Smaller qualitative study helps evaluate and interpret results in a principally QUANTITATIVE study	Smaller quantitative helps evaluate and interpret results in a principally QUALITATIVE study
		Example: A health survey of adolescents with mental health problems reveals ethnic differences. These are followed up with focus groups for parents from different ethnic backgrounds	Example: In-depth interviews with Sam and other adolescent girls reveal a certain narrative pattern to their depression. This is followed up with a brief survey of boys to see if the same pattern may be present
		Adapted from Morgan, 1998	

Practitioner researchers should not feel compelled to use either qualitative or quantitative research methods. Using both in the same research project may be completely logical if the practitioner researcher recognises and identifies the different types of knowledge that they are interested in. By combining the qualitative and quantitative methods practitioner researchers can address the very real multidimensional dilemmas that they face in their everyday practice.

SUMMARY

- There are three different research worlds with which practitioner research is concerned. There is an objective world, a socially constructed world and an individual world
- A wide range of research methods are used to help understand these different worlds. Practitioner researchers need to select the most appropriate method to answer their research questions
- Traditionally, research has been divided into quantitative and qualitative research with little attention to integration in one project
- There are different ways of evaluating quantitative and qualitative research
- Practitioner researchers can combine qualitative and quantitative approaches to research complex multifaceted practitioner issues

FURTHER READING

Robson, C. (2002) *Real World Research*, 2nd edition. Oxford: Blackwell

The second edition of this book provides a comprehensive overview of the issues that face people researching the real world. Despite its size, the book is structured and written in a way that makes it immediately accessible. This should be the bible of any practitioner researcher.

Creswell, J. (2003) *Research Design: Qualitative, Quantitative and Mixed Methods Approaches*. London: Sage

Creswell provides a comprehensive introduction to different types of research for different purposes. However, the main strength of the book is its promotion of using 'mixed methods' when undertaking research in the real world. It is written with clarity and a real understanding of research issues. It is thoroughly recommended for practitioner researchers.

2

Thinking Critically about Theory and Practice

This chapter looks at the complex relationship between professional practice and the assumptions and theories that underpin it. The intention of the chapter is to assist practitioner researchers to think critically about their practice in relation to research ideas. Such critical thinking prior to developing a research proposal will help the practitioner researcher to define relevant theory, and to examine the assumptions underpinning practice, within the framework of the research.

This chapter will include discussion of:

⇨ Professional knowledge
⇨ Propositional knowledge
⇨ Process knowledge
⇨ Personal knowledge
⇨ Value-based knowledge
⇨ Practice culture

2.1 PROFESSIONAL KNOWLEDGE

Schon argues that professionals, such as teachers, nurses and social workers, practice in the 'swampy lowlands' where the 'messy, but crucially important problems' exist (Schon, 1983). In these swampy lowlands, practising professionals work with uncertainty, uniqueness and conflicting values, what Schon (1987) termed the 'indeterminate zones of practice'. He depicts professional

knowledge as not restricted to codified, propositional knowledge but
incorporating the wide scope of knowing essential for professional performance (Eraut, 1994). Understanding this dynamic and complex knowledge
base is intrinsic to examining how practitioner researchers develop and
undertake research into their practice.

Teachers and those working in educational settings encounter children with
reading problems every day. In order to think about how to work most effectively with a child, experienced teachers draw upon different forms of professional knowledge. Several authors (Carper, 1978; Eraut, 1994; Jarvis, 1999)
have attempted to deconstruct professional knowledge. Four intersecting
components have been identified:

- Propositional knowledge: knowledge of content concerns the underlying
  theoretical basis of practice
- Process knowledge: the processes in which professionals engage whilst
  practising
- Personal knowledge: knowledge about self
- Value-based knowledge: moral and ethical values and the beliefs one holds

Application of these components in practice directs the teacher to ask questions such as those outlined in Box 2.1.

Box 2.1 Professional knowledge – teaching reading	
Form of knowledge	**Practice-based questions**
Propositional knowledge	▪ What theory/research is there that might assist me to interpret this child's problem? ▪ What theory/research is there about the best way to teach reading?
Process knowledge·	▪ What practice skills do I possess that will enable me to teach this child to read? ▪ How can I best take account of this child's needs when I work with him/her?
Personal knowledge	▪ What previous experience do I have teaching reading this way? ▪ What previous experience do I have about working with a child like this?
Value-based knowledge	▪ How do I feel about teaching the child reading in this way? ▪ Is this the right thing to do in this situation?

Professional Judgement

Professional judgements on how to teach reading are based on all four areas of knowledge, not simply the evidence base derived from propositional knowledge. The judgements made by professionals are underpinned by an understanding of practice derived through experience. In reality, sufficient propositional knowledge in the form of research being available and accessible is the exception rather than the rule. If a teacher is unable to locate evidence on which to make a judgement he or she makes a professional judgement by integrating the available propositional, process, personal and value-based knowledge.

However, professionals do not practise in isolation, but operate within a context. Within this context the relationship between child, teacher and parents, the classroom, the school and current educational legislation are significant. Judgements occur within this context, and that same context has a profound influence on, and shapes, the judgment of the professional (Martin, 1999).

Applying this to the example above, the teacher may, after assessing the child's needs, develop a teaching strategy for addressing the child's difficulties. In determining the best strategy, the teacher uses his/her personal experience of working with similar children. In addition, the teacher may bring propositional knowledge of the specific learning problems relevant to this child. The teaching strategy is, therefore, designed for a unique child and founded on a unique body of practitioner knowledge.

There are also many conditions occurring within the field of practice that may impact upon such a strategy. These conditions may stem from the socio-political and interpersonal environments. For example, when implementing the reading strategy discussed above the teacher may find that there is little support for innovative practice at the school. He or she is advised that, as a consequence of current education policy, support is only available for certain resources. The best option, based on the teacher's knowledge and experience of practice is, therefore, not available to the child. (For a fuller discussion on professional judgement see Benner et al., 1999; Dowie and Elstein, 1998; Thompson and Dowding, 2002.)

The impact of structures external to the practitioner researcher is dealt with elsewhere in this book. At this point it is important to note that autonomous practice can be limited by the organisation. Where autonomous practice is limited, the practitioner researcher may also find that autonomy within research is equally affected.

Professional Knowledge, Practice and Practitioner Researchers

Experienced practitioners use the different forms of knowledge identified in Box 2.1 to improve practice. Practitioner researchers, undertaking research into practice, also use these different forms of knowledge when developing research proposals. Understanding underlying knowledge about practice is an important precursor to developing research. The following case study describes the impact of these different forms of knowledge on the development of a research proposal by a nurse practitioner researcher.

Case Study:
Angela – professional knowledge in practice

Angela is a nurse who intends to carry out research into oral hygiene as part of an educational course. Angela works in a busy critical care unit in a large general hospital. She works with complex technology and is expected to undertake frequent, specialised, physical interventions on patients. Angela integrates different forms of knowledge in order to function in a nursing role and these same forms of knowledge influence the development of the research proposal.

Propositional knowledge

- The 'body' is a collection of inter-related systems, one or more of which is currently malfunctioning
- The body can be repaired by complex evidence-based clinical procedures undertaken routinely by medical staff
- The malfunctioning body is in a dependent state and nurses ensure continued functioning of all systems during periods of incapacity

Process knowledge

- Patients in dependent states require nurses to meet their needs
- Recovery follows efficient medical diagnosis and physical treatment
- Efficient and competent staff can reassure people in distressed states
- Maintaining working relationships with other members of the team is important for the smooth running of the critical care unit

Personal knowledge

- My role is to support the medical team in saving people's lives
- Caring for people is what I do most effectively
- I role-model good nursing practice for others

Value-based knowledge

- Caring is attending to the needs of physically ill people promptly and efficiently

Angela's initial thoughts about her research are concerned with the delivery of an intervention and the efficacy of that intervention in relation to reducing the incidence of oral hygiene-related problems. This is primarily a view of the research phenomena located in the objective world (see Chapter 1). Angela discusses, in

(Continued)

(Continued)

supervision, how her professional knowledge has shaped her thinking about the research design. Box 2.2 outlines how Angela is assisted by her supervisor to explore other aspects of the phenomena, using the framework discussed in Chapter 1.

Box 2.2 Professional knowledge and research design

Angela's first choice of research design	Alternative designs discussed by Angela and her supervisor during research supervision sessions	
Objective world	Social world	Individually constructed world
Oral hygiene is a procedure for cleaning the mouth cavity and can be evaluated on the basis of reduced incidence of disorders of the oral cavity	Oral hygiene is a procedure undertaken on a person that involves interaction, in some form, between nurse and person. There needs to be a shared understanding to enable the procedure to be carried out effectively	Oral hygiene is an intimate procedure that is a new and unfamiliar experience to most people. As such it will carry unique meaning to individuals. For some people it causes huge anxieties that can result in choking and vomiting

---

Angela's original study design would produce a research project based in the objective world, which would be valuable and worthwhile. However, in considering various approaches Angela challenges her own assumptions about practice and ultimately thinks about other types of valuable research. Whichever she chooses, when reporting her research Angela will be more able to acknowledge that her findings represent only a single view of a highly complex phenomenon.

2.2 PROPOSITIONAL KNOWLEDGE

The case study identified Angela's propositional knowledge as:

- The 'body' is a collection of inter-related systems, one or more of which is currently malfunctioning
- The body can be repaired by complex evidence-based clinical procedures undertaken routinely by medical staff
- The malfunctioning body is in a dependent state and nurses ensure continued functioning of all systems during periods of incapacity

The foundation of professional knowledge has traditionally been a distinctive theoretical model around which propositional knowledge is constructed. The older and 'major professions' such as law, church and medicine, each demarcated a body of knowledge distinct to that single professional group (Glazer, 1974). Critical appraisal of the purpose and implications of such activity is not within the remit of this book; however, readers should refer to Haralambos and Holborn (1991), Gabe et al. (2004) amongst others, for further discussion. Such a discrete body of knowledge is less evident in other professions, such as nursing, social work or teaching (Glazer, 1974). In these professions, practice is primarily an instrumental activity and professionals possess only limited control over propositional knowledge.

A more contemporary view of the foundation of propositional knowledge is that it is a composite, rather than simple, form of knowledge. In Box 2.3, Eraut's (1994) components of propositional or content knowledge are presented and related to Angela's case study.

Box 2.3 Components of propositional knowledge	
Propositional knowledge (Eraut, 1994)	**Angela's propositional knowledge related to the Case Study**
Discipline-based theories and concepts	Micro-biology Homeostatic balance Nutrition Endocrinology Immunology
Generalisations and practical principles	Cleaning of the oral cavity reduces the incidence of opportunistic infection
Specific propositions	If dependent Patient A's oral hygiene is routinely managed, it will promote maintenance of health state and aid recovery

The propositional knowledge that underpins Angela's nursing work is complex. It contains the underlying knowledge of, for example, microbiology, which demonstrates how micro-organisms such as bacteria enter and harm the body. Such knowledge is only valuable if Angela is able to relate this to a practical principle, for example, cleansing to reduce infection. This knowledge is ultimately applied to the individual patient with whom Angela is confronted, Patient A, who is in a dependent state and requires assistance to maintain oral hygiene.

Awareness that professional knowledge is underpinned by propositional knowledge is useful because it provides a route by which the focus of professional attention may be understood. When applied to individual professions it becomes more apparent why the research orientation of, for example, a teacher differs from that of a medical doctor. Figure 2.1 represents the focus of propositional knowledge in different professional groups. The diagram is not intended to represent reality from a micro perspective, but attempts to present a generalised, macro view of the perspective that professional groups have traditionally been presented as holding about the world.

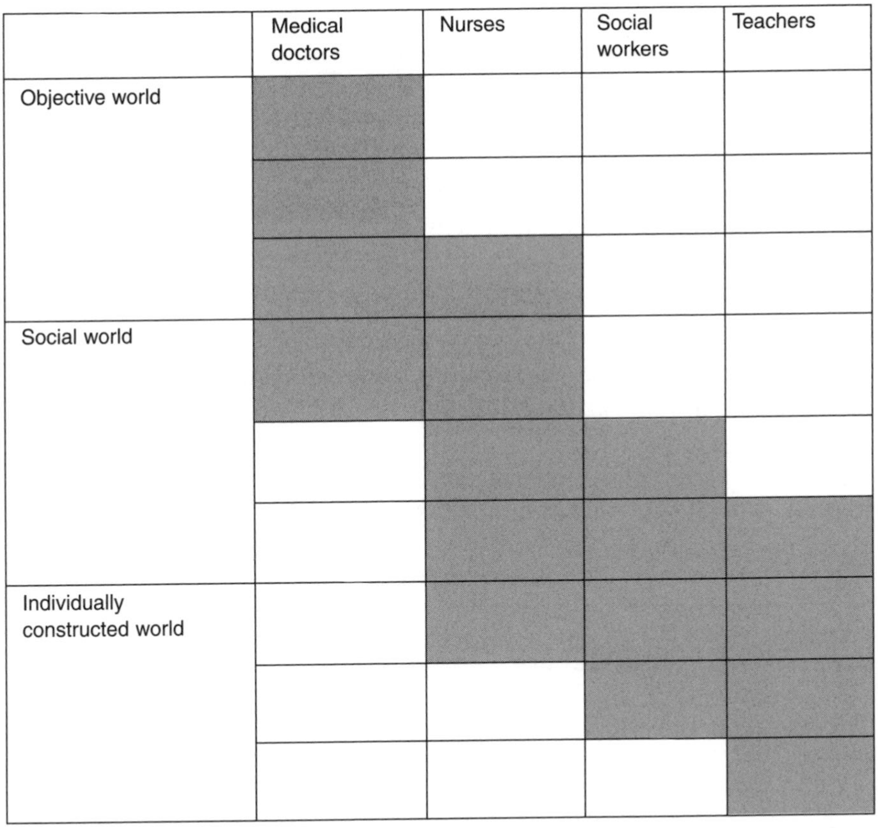

	Medical doctors	Nurses	Social workers	Teachers
Objective world	▓			
	▓			
	▓	▓		
Social world	▓	▓		
		▓	▓	
		▓	▓	▓
Individually constructed world		▓	▓	▓
			▓	▓
				▓

FIGURE 2.1 *Traditional propositional knowledge of professions*

In Figure 2.1 a link is made between propositional knowledge and the three different research worlds outlined in Chapter 1. Where would you place yourself within this framework?

The practitioner researcher's position on the framework may indicate a preference for a particular research design. Understanding this individual preference may be helpful when critically examining research using competing designs. The immediate response may be to reject research findings because they are based upon a particular research world. However, this is a comment on philosophical underpinnings of research rather than research quality as described in Chapter 1. The framework will also, one hopes, trigger further questions. For example:

- Does the underpinning perspective of psychiatric nursing differ from that of learning disability nursing?
- Do psychiatrists share the same understanding of the world as surgeons?
- Do class teachers share the same understanding as head teachers?

Changes to professional education are having a significant impact on the dominance of professionally shaped thinking. For example, higher education institutions that provide healthcare education are employing problem-based learning curricula. Such curricula use 'real world' problems as the basis of student learning. Students are placed within small groups and presented with a 'scenario' consisting of a complex description of a person experiencing a health need. Problem-based learning enables students to develop and use all the forms of knowledge outlined in Box 2.1. The rationale is that this creates professionals who are better prepared to work effectively in contemporary healthcare environments (Glen and Wilkie, 2000). As a consequence there is increasing cross-fertilisation of practice and research perspectives across the professions.

2.3 PROCESS KNOWLEDGE

The case study identified Angela's process knowledge as:

- Patients in dependent states require nurses to meet their needs
- Recovery follows efficient medical diagnosis and physical treatment
- Efficient and competent staff can reassure people in distressed states
- Maintaining working relationships with other members of the team is important for the smooth running of the critical care unit

Knowledge of process is concerned with the practitioner's understanding of the interpersonal aspects of delivering a service. This includes preparation to provide a service, providing the service and evaluating practice.

Practitioners are familiar with the environment in which they work and know how to carry out the various processes that contribute to professional action (Eraut, 1994). Practitioner researchers are also familiar with the environment in which they work, but may be less familiar with research processes. This may mean that the practitioner researcher will find it difficult to think about new ways of doing things. Practitioner researchers may have preconceptions about issues and solutions; these will work against developing an original research design (Robson, 2002). Thus, the practitioner researcher may adopt a questionnaire as the method of data collection simply because that is the method that he or she has used previously. The questionnaire may be the most appropriate method for the particular study, but other methods should be eliminated only following a conscious process of examination and rejection. Consequently, Angela's initial consideration of a research design is a study that is congruent with her understanding of the world in which she works.

Practitioners develop an understanding of the practice environment through prolonged exposure. The experienced practitioner can observe and make sense of complex practice events. Such understanding enables the practitioner to use short cuts to move to the central issue passing beyond the irrelevant data within the field. Schon (1983) describes this as 'naming and framing'. It is a process whereby practitioners name the things to which they will attend and frame the context in which they will be attended to. In a similar way an experienced practitioner researcher can name a practice problem to which attention should be drawn and construct a frame around the problem that will guide and shape the research design. However, for the inexperienced practitioner researcher this can be a problem (see Chapter 11).

Angela names the problem as 'oral hygiene deficit' and frames the problem with 'task', 'bacteria' and 'cleansing'. This name and frame derive from her preconceptions about issues within her practice and will guide selection of a research design. The selected design will be one in which oral hygiene deficit can be examined within the frame of task, bacteria and cleansing. A compatible design might be one that is experimental where the cleaning is measured to see what effect it has on the level of bacteria.

2.4   PERSONAL KNOWLEDGE

The case study identified Angela's personal knowledge as:

- My role is to support the medical team in saving people's lives.
- Caring for people is what I do most effectively
- I role-model good nursing practice for others

The work of Mezirow (1991) is primarily concerned with learning and the adult learner, but is relevant in the context of this chapter. Mezirow's work offers practitioner researchers a framework through which they might deconstruct their unique understanding and assumptions about practice.

Mezirow argues that adult learners struggle to liberate themselves from assumptions developed and strengthened, by various means, from birth onwards (Mezirow, 1991). If adult learners do not challenge the assumptions that underpin their actions they will only be able to function within narrow parameters and persistently make similar mistakes. Intrinsic to examining personal assumptions are 'meaning perspectives' and 'meaning schemes' (see Box 2.4).

Box 2.4   Meaning perspectives and schemes

Meaning perspective	Which generate	Meaning schemes	Which shape	
The structure of assumptions within which one's past experience assimilates and transforms new experience (Mezirow, 1991)	⟶	The particular knowledge, beliefs, value judgements and feelings that become articulated in an interpretation (Mezirow, 1991)	⟶	Research proposals developed by practitioner researchers in practice settings

---

Case Study:
Angela (continued) – making meaning

One of Angela's meaning perspectives about her work is that, in order to care for people, nurses need practice, rather than academic, skills. This meaning perspective has been shaped by, for example:

- A childhood during which her mother, a dynamic general nurse, ministered to neighbours and friends who were unwell
- Socialisation into nursing in a hospital where tradition, and obedience to medical staff, were considered important

(Continued)

(Continued)

The meaning schemes by which Angela articulates this meaning perspective are:

- The patient is dependent
- Caring for, rather than with, patients
- Principal attention to the physical needs of patients
- Maintenance of an efficiently run ward
- Responsiveness to authority

Consequently, Angela's intentions concerning her research are to undertake a study of a nursing procedure where the patient is regarded as an object to be studied with outcomes measured in terms of objective evidence. A study designed in such a way would probably produce outcomes useful:

- To Angela, in enabling her to complete her educational programme
- To the environment in which the research was carried out by confirming the importance of oral hygiene in nursing (a comparatively well researched subject – see for example Evans, 2001)
- To Angela's colleagues by confirming the importance of a procedure
- To Angela's clients by the maintenance of good oral hygiene

However, by sensitive examination of Angela's meaning perspectives and schemes, she might design a wholly original piece of research that would challenge the status quo within the care environment: for example, an exploration of how relatives might be empowered to support service users in maintaining oral hygiene.

The discussion between Angela and her supervisor, presented earlier, examined her assumptions about research. Practitioner researchers should engage in a similar exercise to ensure that they are not limited in their choice of research design.

☐ What are your own meaning perspectives about research? These perspectives may have contributed to the design of previous research studies or to one in which you are presently involved.

☐ What sort of research particularly interests you and why? Can you identify from where these ideas derive?

2.5 VALUE-BASED KNOWLEDGE

The case study identified Angela's value-based knowledge as:

• Caring is attending to the needs of physically ill people promptly and efficiently

What the practitioner researcher decides to do in a given situation will be determined by what he or she believes to be the 'right' thing to do. For example, when confronted with a swamp, an engineer might examine how the swamp could be drained, whilst an ecologist might examine how it might be preserved – neither can be said to be wrong.

Professional practice is underpinned by the judgements that professionals make based upon value-based knowledge. A teacher of reading may be confronted daily with a very basic equation:

$$\text{Time available per student} = \frac{\text{Children in the class}}{\text{Available teaching hours}}$$

Where one child has a specific need that can be addressed through teaching, the teacher may make a value-based judgement and decide that it is right to dedicate additional time to a single pupil. The teacher makes this judgement, taking account of propositional, process and personal knowledge, based upon what he or she believes to be right. The consequence of this decision will mean that the other pupils will receive less than the average time from the teacher.

Ethics, morals, values and beliefs are deeply embedded in the thinking of practitioners (Eraut, 1994). Practitioners engage in practice with the confidence that what they are doing is right. Challenging this belief may damage their ability to function.

Practitioners' confidence in doing the right thing is supported by espousing the ethical stance described within the code of conduct of their professional regulatory bodies. The Nursing and Midwifery Code of Professional Conduct (NMC, 2004), for example, is used to monitor and maintain the standard of nursing practice in the UK. Paragraph 7 of this code states, 'As a registered nurse, midwife or specialist community public health nurse, you must act to identify and minimise the risk to patients and clients.' Angela's practice was underpinned by the following assumption: 'Oral hygiene is a procedure for cleaning the mouth cavity and is evaluated on the basis of reduced incidence of disorders of the oral cavity' (see Box 2.2). This would be suitable evidence of concern to reduce risk to patients and be in accordance with the NMC code of conduct.

Knowledge of morality, however, goes beyond simply knowing the norms or ethical codes of the discipline (Carper, 1978). It includes all voluntary actions that are deliberate and subject to the judgement of right or wrong. Using Carper's assumptions about this area of knowledge, Angela may need to examine her understanding of her own practice, and implicitly the role and function of the nurse within the critical care unit in which she works, as a deliberate activity done to dependent others.

Angela's value-based knowledge is built upon her intention to attend to the needs of physically ill people promptly and efficiently. This will impact upon her research design. Angela's objective is to improve the quality of oral hygiene for her patients. A study that is predicated on improving a task undertaken by nurses on patients would be in accordance with Angela's value base. Research that examined the interaction between nurses and people, or the person's experience of oral hygiene, would be of less importance to Angela since the benefits of such studies would be felt less immediately.

For practitioner researchers, examining the basis of their value-based knowledge requires a supportive environment and supervision (see Chapter 11). It is essential to ensure that practitioner researchers do not ignore this area of professional development, but are supported and guided to recognise the impact that it might have on their research designs.

2.6 PRACTICE CULTURE

So far, examination of the development of the research design has focused primarily on the practitioner researchers' different forms of professional knowledge. The practitioner researcher is not alone within the research environment. Other people will have as great an impact on the research design as Angela's professional knowledge. This culture is:

- Focused on diagnosis, physical treatment and the 'body' as a collection of inter-related systems
- One where patients are generally unable to communicate their needs verbally
- Driven by the need to deliver services promptly and efficiently
- Concerned with maintaining good working relationships between members of the multiprofessional team

Box 2.5 presents a force field analysis of Angela's research. Force field analyses assume that organisations come into stable state at a point where opposing forces are equal (Lewin, 1951). The forces acting on stable state are power-based and derive from political, economic, social and technological domains. Change occurs when the forces for change exceed those for stability. It is acknowledged that Box 2.5 is founded on significant generalisations about practitioners and simplified standpoints.

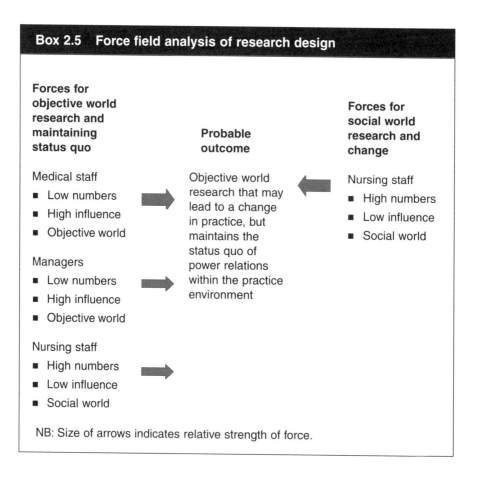

Box 2.5   Force field analysis of research design

Forces for objective world research and maintaining status quo

Probable outcome

Forces for social world research and change

Medical staff
- Low numbers
- High influence
- Objective world

Managers
- Low numbers
- High influence
- Objective world

Nursing staff
- High numbers
- Low influence
- Social world

Objective world research that may lead to a change in practice, but maintains the status quo of power relations within the practice environment

Nursing staff
- High numbers
- Low influence
- Social world

NB: Size of arrows indicates relative strength of force.

It should be noted from Box 2.5 that the arrows relating to nursing staff are present in both right and left columns. This is to indicate that the nursing team may not share a single view of the world and these forces effectively cancel each other out.

A research design that is built on the dominant propositional knowledge in the field deepens understanding of the subject of the research. However, it maintains the status quo by not challenging the current structure of knowledge within the field. Alternatively, the phenomena within the field may be studied using a contrasting design. Such a design would develop new understandings and insights into the subject of the research. It would broaden the area of study by recognising the complexity of research involving people. For the practitioner researcher, others within the field may see openly challenging dominant propositional knowledge as subversive. There are risks associated with practitioner research in terms of destabilisation and the potential backlash if institutional power bases are challenged (McNiff, 2000). Practitioner researchers need to familiarise themselves with such institutional power bases and incorporate strategies to limit their impact both on the practitioner researcher and within the design. This is discussed in detail in Chapter 4.

Case Study:
Angela *(continued)* – **the culture of practice**

Angela indicates to her colleagues and her manager that she intends to undertake research to examine 'communication between nurse and patient during oral hygiene'.

- Angela's manager may see examining communication as an unnecessary interference in the smooth running of the ward that may ultimately lead to slowing down the completion of the task in an already busy environment
- Angela's nursing colleagues may see the expectation that they will communicate with patients as an additional burden requiring specialist skills currently not possessed by the team
- Angela's inter-professional colleagues may see communicating, as an aspect of caring, as eroding the power relations that exist within the clinical area by nurses' adopting a role not directly related to medical diagnosis
- The service users within Angela's area of work may feel that, being in a state of ill health, they would prefer to maintain a passive stance rather than become participants in a study for which they would be required to engage in some manner

Angela, as an autonomous professional, may choose to acknowledge, but not respond to any of these positions. It is her responsibility to produce a research proposal that is coherent, systematic and makes the case for undertaking the research in a particular manner. The governance systems for research may provide Angela with support from outside the clinical area to address the issue. External review may support a proposal that explores a topic from an original perspective, rather than one similar to, or replicating, previous studies. However, working within a team she will need to be aware that alternative views exist and will need to be considered when implementing research findings.

Angela needs to determine whether the benefits of studying communication during oral hygiene outweigh challenging the status quo within the clinical environment. Potentially there would be a number of benefits emerging from such a study, for example:

- Increasing partnership by opening up a dialogue between nurse and client whereby other issues could be raised
- Reducing dependency by providing the opportunity for the nurse to explore with clients how much they are capable of undertaking for themselves
- Improving delivery of oral hygiene by opening up communication for patients to comment on the quality of the procedure

This book aims to develop the status of practitioner research. In order to retain their privileged status within society practitioners have an obligation to strive continually to improve the experience and outcomes for service users. Carrying out research within the field in order to promote change and development is one way in which this obligation can be discharged. Practitioner researchers, who challenge the dominant propositional knowledge in the research field through practice and research, ensure that that field does not become stagnant. Where professionals do not challenge practice, practice can become habituated and ritualistic. Practitioners should be able to think creatively about problems rather than feeling themselves powerless to change behaviours and practice (Jarvis, 1999). Research of practitioner researchers that challenges the status quo can be a powerful incentive to others to recognise that practice is a dynamic activity that should be subject to constant critical appraisal.

SUMMARY

- The professional knowledge of practitioner researchers is a compound of propositional, process, personal and value-based knowledge. An awareness of all these components is important for practitioner researchers seeking to undertake research in practice
- Practitioner researchers should be prepared to place themselves outside practice in order to understand the propositional knowledge driving practice within the research field
- Practitioner researchers should be aware of how the environment, and those within that environment, can overtly and covertly influence the practitioner researcher's selected research design
- Practitioner researchers should seek the support of a research supervisor who will challenge their understanding of practice

FURTHER READING

Eraut, M. (1994) *Developing Professional Knowledge and Competence.* **London: Routledge-Falmer**

Eraut's book represents an overview of the knowledge base of professionals. The work provides the reader with a clear view of how knowledge is developed and used within public services.

Mezirow, J. (1991) Transformative Dimensions of Adult Education. San Francisco: Jossey–Bass

Mezirow, in this and other works, has provided a landscape for the growth and development of professionals. The work argues that current actions should be understood critically within the context of the person.

3

Using Research as a Process for Development

In the previous chapter the importance of practitioners challenging the dominant propositional knowledge in their field was introduced. This chapter develops this by examining the connection between research and development in organisations. A critical distinction is made between change and development and the issues this raises for practitioner research. Types of research that are explicitly devised to ensure development are explored in some depth. Finally, the importance of practitioners using research to change themselves is outlined. The discussion focuses on:

⇨ Development in organisations
⇨ Research designs that promote initiation of change
⇨ Action research designs to promote implementation and continuation
⇨ Action research as social management
⇨ Participatory action research
⇨ Emancipatory research

3.1 DEVELOPMENT IN ORGANISATIONS

Much has been written about the present pace of change in the public sector (see, for example, Fullan, 2001 on change in education). Anyone working in the public sector in the past ten years in the UK will talk about the number of initiatives there have been to ensure change in their service. Central government, regional centres, local governments and individual institutions are constantly trying to introduce change into health, social services and education. Depending on where people are in the system they may feel overwhelmed by the amount of change or on the other hand feel nothing has changed. For example, there have been significant changes in the way GPs are organised and funded. However, for many people their own visits to a GP are virtually indistinguishable from visits made 20 years ago. One is oblivious to these changes from the outside but practitioners on the inside may experience these changes as enormous. Practitioners have had their lives disrupted through stress or redundancy or enhanced by empowerment or promotion by these ongoing changes. Research that is involved in change enters a highly charged personal and professional arena.

Practitioners' response to change can be partly explained by making a distinction between change and progress (see Fullan, 2001). This difference has been recognised for a long time:

> We trained hard, but it seemed that every time we were beginning to form into a team we would be reorganised. I was to learn later in life that we tend to meet any new situation by re-organising, and a wonderful method it can be for creating the illusion of progress, while producing confusion, inefficiency and demoralisation. Caius Petronius (AD 66)

Change does not necessarily improve services. In education the introduction of the National Curriculum in England in the 1990s was a massive change. However, many educators did not see these changes as development in terms of an improvement in the education of young people. Many teachers actively resisted the introduction of the National Curriculum and believed that they were being progressive through resisting change. Similarly, social services reorganisation into specialist teams was resisted by many social workers who felt that this change was not progress. The opposition to these changes affected their implementation.

These aspects of change, its value and whether it is implemented or not, can be represented on a grid (see Figure 3.1).

What practitioner researchers should aim for is Cell 1 in Box 3.1 – change that is of value that is actually implemented. Unfortunately, all too often what happens in the public services is that a change that is of value is not actually implemented (Cell 3) or a change that has no value is implemented (Cell 2). Paradoxically, Cell 4 is equally helpful – a change that is of no value is not implemented (see Fullan, 2001).

Research can help the practitioner achieve Cell 1 – change that is of value actually implemented. It can do this by providing research that helps with:

		Change actually implemented	
		YES	NO
Change of value	YES	1	3
	NO	2	4

FIGURE 3.1 *The value of change*

- The process of change
- Evaluating the outcomes of the change

   This chapter outlines research paradigms that help with the process of change. Evaluation of change is dealt with in Chapter 4.

Stages of Change

Change is a process, not a one-off event. Development in services can be seen as a four-stage process (Fullan, 2001) (see Box 3.1).

Box 3.1   Stages of change

1 **Initiation**: the process that leads to and includes the decision to adopt the change
2 **Implementation:** the first attempt to put the change into practice
3 **Continuation:** whether the change gets built into the organisation/service or disappears
4 **Outcome:** what actually happens as a result of the change

---

   There are multiple changes going on at any one time for the practitioner. Changes (just like buses) do not come along in a neatly spaced sequences. Practitioners are often asked to become involved in research that is part of a process of change. Practitioner researchers need to understand and locate themselves within the change process described in Box 3.2. Is the area they are being asked to research at the initiation stage, the implementation and continuation stage, or the outcome stage of a change? Different stages call for different types of research.

3.2 RESEARCH DESIGNS THAT PROMOTE INITIATION OF CHANGE

Change can be initiated for a number of reasons and at a number of levels (see Fullan, 2001).

- At a government level change can be initiated through new policies. Often such changes are linked to funding. So organisations are invited to bid for money to implement the change
- Change can be initiated for career advancement. Ministers, managers and practitioners are expected to introduce changes. These are often tied to targets or standards. The meeting of standards and introducing new standards becomes a rationale for change for both the individual through performance review and organisations through inspection
- Change can be introduced to cope with other problems. For example, the introduction of testing pupils' attainment in school through SATS was not to improve pupils' learning but to identify failing schools
- Finally, change can be introduced to solve real individual or institutional prob-lems. Practitioners who are concerned about their quality of care to the elderly can change their practice. The manager who is concerned about the quality of care at an institutional level can initiate changes in roles or responsibilities

Whatever the reason or level of the initiation the practitioner researcher should ask one fundamental question at this stage:

'What is the research evidence that underpins this initiative?'

The evidence may come from the variety of types of research as outlined in Chapter 1. Though there is not a direct correspondence between the size of the change and the type of research, there needs to be some link. By questioning what research evidence there is, the practitioner researcher can begin to ensure that research contributes to decisions made about the initiation of the change.

For the practitioner researcher involved in a new service initiative a number of research opportunities will present themselves. These may be either qualitative or quantitative research depending on the questions that need to be answered.

Excluded Pupils Project – A government initiative

The government decides to introduce a new support project for children in danger of being excluded from schools. You are a professional in this new service, which is designed to operate in a multi-agency way.

☑ What research could you undertake to support this new initiative?

Different practitioners, social workers, health visitors or teachers will have different ideas about what is the best way to set up this support service. The issue is not that they are different but rather what research evidence is there that they might be helpful. As this is a national initiative it is not unreasonable to start by asking about the government's research that underpins this change. The government's research may simply be on the size of the problem, that is, the rise in the number of children excluded from schools. It is possible that there may be no research on the solution to the problem (the setting up of the support service).

The government may be keen for research to evaluate the success of the project. For the practitioner researcher, however, the research issue is much more immediate. It is at the initiation stage – what is the best way to set up and operate this new service?

Whatever the reasons for initiation, there are four characteristics to move from this stage to implementation (Fullan, 2001). By focusing research on these four characteristics the practitioner researcher will help move the project towards the next stage of change – implementation.

Need

People must see the need for the change. Research that highlights the need in terms of the size of the problem, the effect on teachers, the effect on the pupil or the family may help this process. One starting point for the practitioner researcher would be to undertake a piece of quantitative research to see how the national figures translate into local figures for exclusion. Such a comparison might well confirm the need or otherwise for this new service.

Clarity

People are often not clear how they are meant to do things differently. Policies are often vague and it is left to local managers to implement. In this example research that clarifies how the new service will meet the needs of the teachers will be helpful at the initiation stage. So a survey of head teachers to understand the different reasons for excluding children would be one strategy.

Complexity

The change required is often multifaceted. In this example it requires the setting up of a multi-agency team followed by the delivery of a new service to a large number of separate organisations (schools). Research suggests that complex changes are often more effective than simple ones (Fullan, 2001). This is especially true if the complex change can be broken down into incremental steps. Research that recognises these steps is helpful, so research might focus on how the issue of exclusion is socially constructed differently by schools and parents.

Practicality

Many changes are politically driven and often at the initiation stage the material is not available to implement the programme. Research that focuses on developing workable material may be vital to the implementation and continuation of the programme. For example, practitioner research might undertake phenomenological research to see how pupils who have been recently excluded view the triggers to their exclusion. This could be the start of developing training material for teachers to recognise and handle these particular trigger points successfully.

By knowing about the characteristics of successfully initiating change, practitioner researchers can focus their research efforts. By doing so it is more likely that the change will move to the next two stages – those of implementation and continuation.

3.3 ACTION RESEARCH DESIGNS TO PROMOTE IMPLEMENTATION AND CONTINUATION

The second stage of the change process is when the project begins to be implemented. Many good new ideas for change will never get even to this stage. For those that do, only a small number will develop and grow. There are some powerful research paradigms that can be used to help this process. These methods may use quantitative and/or qualitative methods for gathering and analysing data. However, they approach research from a different perspective to the quantitative and qualitative paradigms discussed in Chapter 1. Essentially these research paradigms are about actually using the research process to support change and development.

   These research paradigms can be grouped under the umbrella heading of 'action research' to emphasise the change nature of them all. However, some come from very different backgrounds than the traditional action research model, and even action research is described in a variety of ways (see Rearick and Feldman, 1999). They all have a particular perspective on the best methods of implementation and continuation of change as well as how change should be initiated.

Box 3.2   Three action research paradigms

1. Action research as rational social management
2. Participatory action research
3. Emancipatory research

In addition there is a fourth action research paradigm, developed by education researchers, known specifically as practitioner research (Hollingsworth, 1997; McGinnis, 2001). Practitioner research is a self-reflective method, which is explored in Chapter 5.

These three action research paradigms are interlinked (Kemmis and Wilkinson, 1998). All of them explicitly recognise that research is about power and that traditionally the researcher had the power and the researched were powerless. In this way, traditionally research reinforced the researchers' power by giving their view more validity than those of the people being researched. The different paradigms of action research try to address this by giving power back to the researched.

These action research paradigms are a means by which the practitioner researcher acknowledges and uses the power contained within the research process to facilitate change. Research is informed by political agendas of the individual, the organisation and the government. The issue in action research is how it can empower the researcher and the researched. This empowerment can be for the participants in the research, the organisation in which they work or for the researcher (see Creswell, 2003).

Action research has, at best, ambiguous standing in the research world. In the academic world it has a limited standing. Some would cynically suggest that this is because many academics are not interested in research that resolves applied problems in organisations. Action research is also seen as rejecting a positivist paradigm that has dominated medical research. For many medical researchers it is therefore seen as rather second-rate and not deserving the status of research (see Hart and Bond, 1996). The main problem, however, is that action research covers such a broad field that there is great confusion about what it is and what it is not. Critics argue that it is difficult to define what good quality action research is. This is a fair criticism in so far as action research, as an umbrella term, covers a number of areas. In the same way that qualitative research and quantitative research cover a whole raft of methods, so does action research. Action research embraces those research methodologies whose central feature is one of change. Central to its validity therefore is whether it has helped with the process of change.

3.4   ACTION RESEARCH AS SOCIAL MANAGEMENT

Kurt Lewin's seminal paper (1946) 'Action research and minority problems' describes the process of action research as one that ties together a systematic, preferably an experimental, approach to a social problem with social action to resolve it. He contrasted traditional research that tried to develop theories about general laws of life and action research that used theory to look at specific problems in organisations or situations. Lewin was specifically interested in using group dynamics not only to explain the problems in organisations but also to develop the research process.

This tradition of action research is of particular interest to practitioner researchers because the focus is on resolving problems using applied aspects of a traditional scientific approach to research.

Maruyama (1996) has outlined key aspects of Lewin's action research that appeal to the traditional researcher:

- The strength that comes from combining quantitative and qualitative data
- The importance of careful observation
- The value of recording scientifically the essential happenings during an intervention as part of the evaluation of its effectiveness
- The necessity of doing action research without lowering standards of validity and reliability found in more 'microscopic' research

Action research sees change as requiring rational solutions to technical problems. The belief is that problems can be understood by collecting accurate data on them. When the data are analysed the practitioners in an organisation will be in a better position to understand the problems and therefore to change how they work. This type of action research, as rational social management, is particularly appropriate for practitioner researchers in management positions trying to ensure that change is implemented. The research paradigm is based on four features (see Box 3.3).

Box 3.3   Four features of action research as rational social management

- A cyclical process
- The researcher is an active participant
- Doing things differently
- The research participants are active

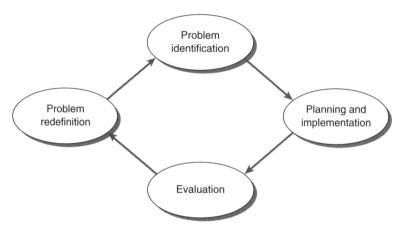

FIGURE 3.2 *Action research as a cyclical process*

A Cyclical Process

Action research is essentially defined as a cyclical process (see Figure 3.2). The first stage is problem identification and deciding on the objective for the change (including fact finding about the problem). The second stage consists of planning and implementation an intervention to reach the objective. This intervention is then evaluated. Finally, the problem is redefined and the cycle begins anew.

An example of action research as rational social management with the Excluded Pupils Project is given below.

Case Study:
Excluded Pupils Project – rational social management

Tom is the service manager of the new Excluded Pupils Project. It is Tom's responsibility to ensure that it is implemented. He decides to use his weekly team meetings to start an action research project to support the implementation strategy.

- **Problem identification:** At the first team meeting Tom asks the team to keep diaries of the critical incidents that get in the way of successful working
- **Planning and intervention:** After a month he collects the diaries and analyses them. Tom uses a thematic analysis of the types of issues that came up. This is coded and scored according to seriousness of the problem and the most common issues are identified. He then introduces three strategies that

(Continued)

(Continued)
> he thinks might alleviate the problem. Each member of the team is allocated a particular way of dealing with the problem
> - **Evaluation of action:** For the next month each team member implements their allocated strategy. Diary records are again kept and at the end of the month Tom re-analyses them
> - **Problem redefined:** On the basis of this analysis Tom identifies which strategy is best for dealing with this problem. He informs the team and then decides on a new problem for attention

The Researcher is an Active Participant

Action research ensures the researcher is an active participant in the research process. In action research as rational social management the practitioner researcher (Tom, in our example) is still seen, in the traditional sense, as an expert research consultant. The practitioner researcher may be from within the same organisation but often a different department or section. The practitioner researcher is seen as bringing expertise in research methodology and in theoretical perspectives. This expertise is then shared with the participants who are recognised as experts in their own situation. The research process is seen as a collaborative partnership. Within this partnership there is recognition of the differences in values and power of the people involved. The active participation of the researcher fits with the practitioner researcher model. The difficulty is that the practitioner researcher is often not seen as having the expertise in research that allows him or her to play this role in their own organisation.

Doing things differently

The purpose of action research as rational social management is not simply to generate new knowledge. The purpose is for the research participants to solve a problem they have in the workplace and to do things differently.

> If we cannot judge whether an action has led forwards or backward, if we have no criteria for evaluating the relationship between effort and achievement, there is nothing to prevent us from making the wrong conclusions. (Lewin, 1946: 202)

In the Excluded Pupils Project it is expected that the team members will act differently once they have researched the most effective methods of tackling a particular issue. The actual undertaking of the research is seen as part of the process of change.

The research participants are active

The research participants are actively involved in the research and the research process. They may well be involved in the identification of the problem as well as collecting the data. As data are analysed there is feedback to all participants. However, as we will see below, the involvement of the participants is still much more limited in the rational social management paradigm than in the other action research models.

One of the difficulties for practitioner researchers undertaking traditional action research is that often the research ends at the completion of the first cycle rather than continuing into the next cycle. This may be because the research frame is time-limited and managers (or academic institutions) need a fixed point of ending. This goes against one of the major reasons for undertaking action research, that is the recognition that development in organisations is a process that takes time.

3.5 PARTICIPATORY ACTION RESEARCH (PAR)

Right from Lewin's earliest papers, the model of action research as rational social management was used in education (see for example Corey, 1953) and by the 1970s it was developing in new and exciting ways in the UK (Carr, 1989). Elliott's (1978) paper 'What is action research in schools?' challenged the distinction between researchers and practitioners and between theory and practice that was being made at this time. This message was reinforced by Kemmis (1982), who argued that the solution to problems (in this case educational) would not come from distant expert academic researchers but rather from practitioners, reflecting on and researching their own practice either individually or as a critical community or network. New ways of undertaking action research were developed to try to connect theory and practice. Central to this was removing the distinction between practitioner and researcher. The importance of being both a practitioner and a researcher was strengthened. These approaches became known as 'participatory action research' (PAR).

Collaboration between people is seen as the central feature of participatory action research:

> A distinctive feature of participatory action research is that those affected by planned changes have the primary responsibility for deciding on courses of critically informed action which seem likely to lead to improvement, and for evaluating the results of strategies tried out in practice. (McTaggart, 1994: 317)

In PAR the researcher moves from the role of being the expert in research to that of a process facilitator. The researcher is no longer centre stage deciding on how the research should be carried out. Instead their role is to help participants with the process of research. This process is essentially the cyclical research process elaborated in Figure 3.2 (on page 50).

Case Study:
Excluded Pupils Project – participatory action research

Tom is the service manager of the new Excluded Pupils' Project. He decides to use PAR to help with the implementation. Because he realises that his own position as manager may get in the way he invites the team to nominate a practitioner researcher from another part of the organisation to lead the process. They nominate Ben.

Ben joins the team for their weekly team meeting. He identifies with them the stumbling blocks to successful implementation. They decide to keep diaries for a month. At the end of the month Ben introduces a number of different ways that the diaries can be analysed. The team chooses to undertake a narrative analysis of the diaries. Ben continues to facilitate the team's research. They complete the action cycle but this time they decide on the next step.

One of the prime requirements for the researcher, as process facilitator, is to establish trust within their group or research community. At the start there needs to be recognition that not everyone in the action research group will see the same thing as a problem to be sorted out. In other words, the group who are involved in the research need to create a shared meaning for an event as a precursor to researching it.

The purpose of the research is usually exploratory rather than experimental. The design of the research then needs to be socially constructed. Data are collected in the organisation using such methods as participant observation, interviews and the analysis of documentary evidence. Data are more likely to be validly collected if research participants agree on why it is being collected in this way.

Quantitative and qualitative data as well as self-reflection are seen as valid. Data are validated by a process of triangulation, participant confirmation and by testing the coherence of arguments (McTaggart, 1994). Data are also validated by participants' willingness not only to disseminate information but also to change practice. In this way, for the most pragmatic reasons, it is recognised that the better the collaboration, the more likely people will implement the changes that come out of the research.

Maruyama (1996) has highlighted a number of reasons for this shift from action research as rational social management to PAR (see Box 3.4).

Box 3.4   The attractions of participatory action research

Ownership

Practitioners and managers are usually interested in improving their own services rather than providing generalisations to other similar organisations around the country. Practitioners and managers therefore feel more ownership of the research and more confident to say something about their own situation precisely because it is not intended for generalisations to other areas.

Research as part of practice

Research is seen as less of a specialised area but one in which many practitioners have some skills and knowledge. Most undergraduate and postgraduate courses in health, education and the social sciences will contain some teaching of research methodologies.

Research to improve practice

Practitioners are less worried about having a theoretical framework to make sense of the results but rather want results that make sense in their practical context. They want practical theory.

Control

Practitioners want control over the research process. This means that they do not become dependent on the researcher. More importantly, more practitioners become engaged in research.

For practitioner researchers PAR is very attractive. It allows the organisation to be a central part of the research process. It ensures that colleagues are directly engaged in research and allows the practitioner researcher to facilitate the process of the research.

For some engaged in PAR the approach is explicitly for use with groups or communities who are oppressed in order to bring about fundamental social change (Brydon-Miller, 2001). So PAR might be used with people with mental health issues or with disabilities, and with school children. However, a third research paradigm has also been developed specifically to address the issues of disempowered groups.

3.6 EMANCIPATORY RESEARCH

Emancipatory research moves PAR a step further. It is critical of other research paradigms' failure to recognise the power imbalance contained in and exacerbated by the research process. Emancipatory research is aimed at research with groups in society who are marginalised and powerless. It is sometimes also known as participatory research or advocacy research as both are core elements of this perspective. There are many types of emancipatory research but they all have in common 'a fundamental interest in emancipation and empowerment to engage in autonomous action arising out of authentic, critical insights into the social construction of human society' (Grundy, 1987: 19). Emancipatory research has a very strong political purpose. It aims to uncover the injustices of the world and show how imbalances are created in society.

Box 3.5   Types of emancipatory research

- **Feminist perspectives:** focus on gender imbalance
- **Racialised discourses:** focus on discourses about colour
- **Queer theory:** focus on the experiences of gay, lesbian, bisexual and transgendered people
- **Disability research:** focus on how the individual and social model of disability create policy

(adapted from Creswell, 2003)

Emancipatory research has developed in a number of areas (see Box 3.5). Each focuses on people who have been marginalised and disempowered by society. The aim of the research is often about ensuring that the knowledge, experiences and perceptions of people from these groups shifts others' (men, white, heterosexual, the able-bodied, practitioners) perceptions but also shifts the perceptions of the marginalised group about themselves. The focus below is on disability research as it clearly illustrates the issues involved in undertaking emancipatory research.

The disability world has seen emancipatory research as significantly different from other research (British Council of Disabled People website www.bcodp.org.uk/about/research). Emancipatory disability research was triggered in the UK by a series of seminars organised by the Joseph Rowntree

Foundation in the 1990s. The concern was on how research in the area of disability was usually characterised by an individual (or medical) model of disability. This model of research focuses on how the person's disability affects their lives. So, for example, there has been a good deal of research on how children with a disability may have a lower self-concept than their able-bodied peers (see Richardson et al., 1964). The objection of people with a disability to the individual model is that the focus for change is always on them – they have to work on overcoming their disability. In contrast, they argue that the focus needs to be on the society in which they live, including the attitudes of the able-bodied. They argue it is society that should be the focus for research, and therefore of change, not themselves. The social model of disability stresses that it is the economic, cultural and environmental barriers that disable some people – and consequently should be the focus of research. This is quite a radical shift as it is saying that at a fundamental level research is political and the focus of the research (the individual with a disability or the society they live in) actually creates the focus for the change.

In our example of the Excluded Pupils Project, emancipatory research would start from the position that it is not the disempowered excluded pupil who needs to change but rather the organisation that has excluded the pupil (see the case study below).

Case Study:
Excluded Pupils Project – emancipatory research

Tom is still the service manager. He decides that it is the excluded pupils and their families that are disempowered and must be involved to make the project work. In consultation with his staff he organises a series of meetings where excluded pupils and their parents come and tell their stories. These stories are taped (with consent). Tom and his team analyse these stories using narrative analysis, and from them certain patterns emerge.

The team shares this information with the pupils and their parents at another meeting. This generates a series of ideas for helping teaching staff realise when they are losing control and are likely to move to an 'exclusion position'.

On the basis of this material Tom and his team (which now includes excluded pupils and their parents) begin a series of workshops in schools for senior members of staff.

The emancipatory research agenda for disability is characterised by seven core principles (see the British Council of Disabled People's website).

- **Control:** People with disability must be involved from the beginning to the end of the research process. Though able-bodied people can carry out the research, they must be accountable to disabled people
- **Accountability:** Research procedures and practice must be open and explained to research participants. Findings must be disseminated in appropriate formats
- **Empowerment:** Research must attempt to leave the disabled people in a better position than before. It must not exploit their situation for the benefit of the researchers
- **The social model of disability:** The focus of the research should be on the economic, cultural and environmental barriers encountered by people
- **The need for rigour:** Researchers must ensure that their research methods are logical, rigorous and open to public and academic scrutiny
- **The choice of methods:** This depends upon the needs of the project. Methods can be either quantitative or qualitative
- **The role of experience:** Research on disabled people's experience should be put within a context in order to highlight the disabling consequences of the focus on a non-disabled majority in society

Emancipatory research does not necessarily follow the cyclical research process of the other action research models. Instead the focus is on ensuring that the research area is that which is important to marginalised groups. Secondly, it ensures that the results of the research are used to bring about positive change for this group of people.

SUMMARY

- Change is a process not an event
- There is a difference between change and progress
- Practitioner researchers need to know where they are located in the four-stage change process of initiation, implementation, continuation and outcome
- If involved in the initiation stage practitioner researchers should address in their research the issues of need, clarity, complexity and quality
- If involved in implementation and continuation practitioner researchers should focus on one of the action research paradigms that connects research and development
- Action research ensures that the research process is an active part of the development in an organisation
- The type of action research practitioner researchers use depends on what they are trying to achieve within an organisation

FURTHER READING

Fullan, M. (2001) *The New Meaning of Educational Change*, **3rd edition. London: Cassell**

This classic text provides a brilliant introduction to how change happens in organisations. The particular examples used are on the education system both here and in North America. However, the lessons drawn are applicable to all institutions within the state system.

McTaggart, R. (1994) 'Participatory action research: issues in theory and practice', *Educational Action Research*, **2 (3): 313–37**

This readable paper sets out the historical background to participatory action research. It stresses the importance of PAR in challenging present structures in society and government. A series of PAR projects from around the world illustrate how the process is about groups of people who need to research together to be able to change themselves, their communities and the wider political system.

4
Evaluating Your Own Organisation

Practitioner researchers can undertake exactly the same sort of research in their own organisation as they would in any other. So the purpose of research can be exploratory or descriptive, explanatory or action research. However, practitioner researchers are often asked to undertake evaluative research in their own organisation. Evaluative research is therefore the main focus of this chapter. In particular, this chapter deals with:

- ⇨ The shadow side of organisations
- ⇨ Working with the shadow side of organisations
- ⇨ Evaluation
- ⇨ Realist evaluation
- ⇨ Undertaking realist evaluation
- ⇨ The shadow side of evaluation

4.1 THE SHADOW SIDE OF ORGANISATIONS

Egan (1994) introduced the importance of understanding and being able to work with the 'shadow side' of organisations for managers. This is equally important for practitioner researchers researching their own organisation. The shadow side means the hidden side of the organisation:

> The shadow side deals with the covert, the undiscussed, the undiscussable, and the unmentionable. (Egan, 1994: 4)

Working with the shadow side highlights the advantages of the practitioner researcher researching their own organisation. The practitioner researcher from inside the organisation will know the shadow side in a way that an external person cannot. This is particularly important if the purpose of the research is evaluative. The internal practitioner researcher can also research the shadow side in their own organisation. In this way it is through research that the shadow side of the organisation is understood. These are the advantages of researching your own organisation. There are also significant difficulties.

Case Study:
The shadow side of researching consent

Elsie worked in an adult psychiatric hospital. The importance of informed consent by patients for treatment is central to the new culture in the NHS. From her work she became aware that discussing treatment options with patients varied considerably from consultant to consultant. Elsie decided that she would research the issue by interviewing ex-patients and hearing their stories about giving consent. This exploratory research was then used as a basis for undertaking semi-structured interviews with consultant psychiatrists. On the basis of this research the shadow side of patients giving informed consent was made public.

The shadow side activities of an organisation are not always negative. Shadow side activities can be helpful and have a value to the organisation. For example, a local authority may have a policy of not sending any children with special educational needs to out-of-county boarding schools; however, everyone working in this area for the local authority knows that there are children in out-of-county boarding schools. The reasons for the out-of-county placements might be valid and positive, but they become part of the shadow side of the local authority because such placements are not acknowledged as happening.

Research issues can be on the shadow side because they are not known about for a number of reasons:

- They are intentionally hidden from others: for example, people hide the fact that they are collecting data because they do not know if their manager would approve
- Not knowing is embedded in the culture of the organisation: for example, data are collected on a wide range of issues but are never analysed
- Naïveté by practitioners: for example, people may simply not understand statistical data and therefore may misunderstand the information placed in front of them

In addition there are some research activities on the shadow side because managers do not want to know about them. This can be summed up by the attitude, 'Don't tell me because then I'll have to act'.

There are five areas of shadow side activities that it is important for the practitioner researcher to understand:

- Organisational culture
- Personal styles
- Organisational social systems
- Organisational politics
- The hidden organisation

Organisational culture

The culture of the organisation is defined as 'the way we do things around here'. The practitioner researcher (you) needs to understand the shadow side of the research culture. The espoused culture may be that research is important.

- ☐ What is the shadow side?
- ☐ When was a research report last circulated?
- ☐ When was a piece of research last actually acted upon?

Personal styles

- ☐ What is the style of the person responsible for the research? Does the research director really promote research or just their own research? Does the manager get along with the research manager? If not, what are the implications for the research?

Organisational social systems

- ☐ Who are the in-groups and the out-groups in research? Where do you sit? How do your relationships change if you call yourself a researcher or a practitioner? Does your team change? What are the implications for undertaking research?

Organisational politics

- ☐ Politics is about power. There are different sorts of power in organisations. Some sorts may be quite open. Other sources of power may be in the shadow side.
- ☐ Who has the power to block the research? Who has the power to protect it?

The hidden organisation

This is the organisation that grows up inside the overt organisation. So there may be a written policy on getting time, or approval, to do research, but everyone inside the organisation will know that there is also a shadow policy. This shadow system may simply consist of walking into the director's office and being clear that the organisation will gain (or could lose) money if permission for this research is not given.

☑   What is the hidden research organisation?

4.2 WORKING WITH THE SHADOW SIDE OF ORGANISATIONS

The complexity of organisations and their shadow side can helpfully be seen as a 'soft' system (Checkland and Scholes, 1990). These authors suggest that there is no hard reality to an organisation. Instead organisations should be seen as complex messy systems that are forever changing.

This complexity can be captured by a 'Rich Picture'. Rich pictures can be used in a variety of ways in research (see Dick and Swepson, 1994). They can be used with the action research and emancipatory research paradigms. They are also a useful technique to develop as a reflective research practitioner (see Chapter 11). The focus here is on understanding the messiness of researching your own organisation and in particular how the shadow side may impact on the research.

Fundamental to this is recognising that people in the organisation will construct different views of the research. These views will reflect:

* People's individual differences, including their background and experience of research
* Their roles and positions in the organisation
* Their expectation that the research will harm or benefit them
* The culture of the organisation

The practitioner researcher's role is to try to understand these different views. The practitioner researcher should try to remain neutral whilst recognising that his or her place in the organisation will affect not only how people see them but also the research that they are about to undertake. One way of clarifying these positions is to ask questions about the stakeholders in the research and the culture of the organisation.

 Think about undertaking some research in your organisation. Start by clarifying who are the various stakeholders in the research.

1   **Who are the stakeholders in the research?**
☑   Who is the **commissioner**? This is the person who asked for the research to happen in the first place.

(Continued)

(Continued)

- ☐ Who are the **service providers**? These are the people who are involved in delivering the service that is going to be researched and who may be directly affected by the results
- ☐ Who are the **service users**? These are the people to whom the service is geared and who should benefit from any improvements or developments

When you have clarified who the stakeholders are, think about the culture of the organisation.

2   What is the culture of the organisation?

Decision-making:
- ☐ How do decisions get made?
- ☐ How do they get implemented?
- ☐ What are the goals and who sets them?

Power:
- ☐ Who has the power in the organisation?
- ☐ How is power used in terms of access to and dissemination of information?
- ☐ Who has influence over budgets?
- ☐ Who has control of meetings?
- ☐ Who has power over key stakeholders?

Practitioner researchers may well have access to most of this information. If not, then they need to ask the above questions before drawing a rich picture.

The rich picture

Organisations can be visually represented through a rich picture (see Checkland and Scholes, 1990). Rich pictures can be drawn by researcher on their own or in consultation with other stakeholders. It is simply an effective way of capturing the complexity of the real world. Artistic skills are not required and there is no right rich picture for any organisation. Instead it is a dynamic way of understanding the context of the piece of research.

Some of the things that it is helpful to capture in a rich picture are:

- The structure of the service/organisation, that is the 'bricks and mortar'
- Process: the activities that go on within the structure
- Interaction between structure and process
- People: who are the dominant people in the service, what they are saying and thinking, how they interact with each other

- Researcher: where they are in the system
- Time: how time is represented

Rich pictures can be drawn in different ways, however there is a conventional set of symbols that is often used (see Figure 4.1).

FIGURE 4.1   *Conventional symbols used in rich pictures*

The point of the rich picture is to see the 'whole picture' including the shadow side of a service or organisation. The picture should illustrate the way in which the proposed research fits into the service or organisation, and how the culture and people in the organisation are going to affect the research. Rich pictures can be drawn in isolation by the researcher, but the best use of rich pictures is to draw them with the stakeholders in the organisation. In this way light is shone on the shadow side of the organisation from a number of perspectives.

Case Study:
Elsie's rich picture of researching consent in a psychiatric hospital

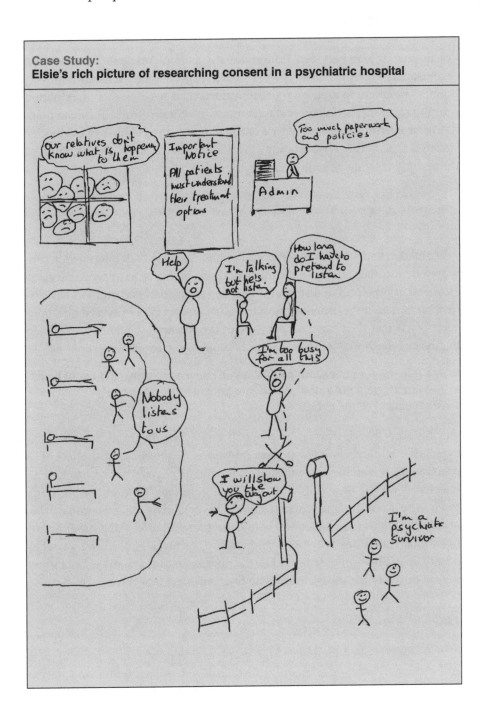

Understanding the shadow side is one of practitioner researchers' great strengths when researching their own organisations. Because they are aware of the organisation's culture, their research is more likely to be successful.

4.3   EVALUATION

Practitioner researchers can undertake any sort of research in their own organisation. However, one type of research is particularly relevant for practitioners researching their own organisations. This is evaluation. Evaluation uses the same methodology and techniques as other research. It can be qualitative or quantitative or a mixture of the two. It is the purpose of evaluative research that is different. Though evaluation can mean a whole range of things, it is essentially about judging the value or worth of something:

> The purpose of an evaluation is to assess the effects and effectiveness of something, typically some innovation, intervention, policy, practice or service. (Robson, 2002: 202)

Evaluation and audit have some similarities. They are both interested in programme outcomes and have a similar purpose in trying to improve services. However, it is helpful to distinguish between evaluation and audit. A key distinction is that audit usually concentrates on answering normative questions such as whether the programme or service is operating as intended and meeting the standards that it has set. So audit would answer such questions as:

- Are referrals for out-patient appointments being seen within the target time?
- Are reports sent out to the appropriate people?
- Are feedback forms collated?

On the other hand, evaluative research has a broader brief. In particular evaluative research is interested in questions about cause and effect. The practitioner researcher is interested in whether the programme has had an effect and why it has. The 'why' question goes way beyond the auditor's brief. Why a programme works (or doesn't work) involves generating a theory that explains the connection between different parts of the programme. In summary, auditing whether a programme has met standards may well be part of an evaluation. A true evaluation goes beyond this limited brief to try to find out why the programme is having the effect that it has.

Types of Evaluation

A distinction is often made between two basic types of evaluation: outcome and process. These are sometimes distinguished as summative and formative evaluation (see Clarke, 1999 for a fuller discussion).

- **Outcome** (summative) evaluation is concerned with the overall effectiveness or impact of a programme or service
- **Process** (formative) evaluation is concerned with understanding the means, or process, by which the programme is being implemented

These two different types of evaluation align themselves more readily with the two different types of research paradigms of qualitative and quantitative research (see Chapter 1).

The purpose of an outcome evaluation is to find out if a programme is effective. This is attractive to people interested in a positivist approach. The research is to show whether the programme is effective and hard data are often required. A 'maybe – sort of' answer is not seen as very helpful. The answer about effectiveness is usually given in numbers – quantitative data. Questions such as how effective, how many and how much are all seen as important. This type of purpose tends to work against a qualitative approach, which is seen as merely representing people's opinions. Unless the data goes beyond this it is not seen as helpful.

On the other hand, the purpose of process evaluation is to find out how the programme is working. Process evaluation is concerned with how people make sense and give meaning to the programme as a way of understanding how it is working. There may be a number of perspectives on this because different people may have different experiences of the programme. There is recognition that the world is socially constructed. This type of evaluation sees qualitative research as particularly useful.

For practitioner researchers, however, a mixed approach is often what is required when understanding how a service operates and why it has an effect.

Practitioner researchers need to be clear about which parts of their evaluation are about outcome and which about process. We can illustrate some of the differences with an example of evaluating a counselling service.

Case Study:
Evaluating a counselling service

Dev's manager wants him to evaluate a new counselling service that has been set up for people with physical disabilities. Dev decides that he needs to clarify a number of issues in order to decide whether an outcome or process evaluation is most appropriate.

Outcome evaluation

At what stage is the service?
Comment. All too often researchers are asked to evaluate a project before it has been running long enough to have had any outcomes. Researchers need to resist

(Continued)

(Continued)

undertaking an outcome evaluation in an inappropriate time span. It may be possible, however, for Dev to set up an outcome evaluation for someone else to complete.

Is it clear what the objectives of the service are?
Comment: There are often multiple objectives for new services. Some of these may be overt and written into documents and some are part of the shadow side of the organisation. In this example one of the overt objectives is to increase clients' independence thus reducing the demands placed on social workers. However, a covert objective of the service is to increase the assertiveness of people with disability – thus paradoxically increasing the demands that they place on social workers. Dev realises there has to be agreement about what are the service objectives for outcome research.

Are there any 'baseline' data on these objectives?
Comment: Service developments are often introduced for a variety of reasons (see Chapter 3 for a full discussion). There are often little or no data on the status quo before the introduction of the new service. Clarifying whether there are any 'baseline data' or previous research is essential. Dev discovers that no data have been kept.

Is there a comparison group?
Comment: In a randomised control trial (as we have seen, the gold standard for quantitative research) the way that people are allocated to receive the service is crucial. For most new services such randomisation is not practical, not ethical and not managed. In our scenario the service has taken on all people with a physical disability that were referred to it. The lack of a comparison group affects the way the service can be evaluated. Dev finds out that there are disabled people who have not received the service. However, this group is not comparable with the people who have.

Process evaluation

Who are the stakeholders?
Comment: There are usually a range of stakeholders in a new service. Dev identifies the stakeholders as the people receiving the counselling service. In addition there are other significant people such as partners and extended family of the client as well as the social workers who had originally made the referral. In addition there are the views of the people actually delivering the services – the counsellors.

What part of the process is it important to evaluate?
Comment: The obvious answer is the quality of the counselling – after all that is what this service is primarily about. However, there are other parts of the process that could also be evaluated. One of these is the decision-making process of the social workers when referring people with disabilities.

These six questions highlight the areas that practitioner researchers need to think about. However, behind them are the shadow aspects of the organisation that also need to be kept in mind – in this case the manager's desire for an outcome evaluation, despite the lack of time that the service has been running. It therefore could not be ignored by Dev and the following evaluation was devised.

For the outcome evaluation, quantitative standardised data were required so the CORE (Clinical Outcomes in Routine Evaluation) Outcome Measure was given to each client when they were referred and after they had their final counselling session. The CORE Outcome Measure is a patient self-report instrument that assesses in standardised form the psychosocial domains of subjective well-being, problem symptoms, functioning and risk (see Evans et al., 2000). In addition, the uniqueness of each client was recognised. So each client agreed their own objectives for counselling at the start of the sessions. They were then asked to evaluate their progress against each of their own objectives at the end of counselling.

For the process evaluation, semi-structured interviews were undertaken with each client to ascertain the quality of the counselling. In addition, focus groups for clients and carers as well as one for social workers were run. A further focus group was run using disabled people who had not been referred. Their role was to help make meaning out of the qualitative information that the other focus groups had provided.

[*Postscript*: Was the evaluation of the service successful? Yes. Scores on the CORE battery went down, client objectives were largely achieved. Why was it effective? Because clients, families and social workers felt supported (a counselling cliché, we know). However the real success of the evaluation was on the shadow side. The managers of the service who were initially sceptical of the value of counselling for people with disability became much more understanding and supportive of this service.]

Evaluation of a service is rarely as simple as saying that it works, or it does not work. Combining outcome and process evaluation addresses some of that complexity.

4.4 REALIST EVALUATION

In recent years a new way to think about evaluation has been developed which appears to be an important way forward for practitioner researchers. Realist evaluation fundamentally challenges the split between positivist and social constructionist research.

Realism in research has developed from the thinking of Bhaskar (1975) and Harré (1972) and has more recently found expression in evaluation in the work of Pawson and Tilley (1997). The realist paradigm is also known as post-positivism, critical realism and generative realist (Matthews, 2003). It takes a radically different view on research to those of positivism and social constructionism and many would argue it is the way of moving forward on the paradigm debate as it combines a scientific way of thinking with recognition of the context and uniqueness of human behaviour. There are also elements of emancipatory research, as it recognises the importance of the individual perspective (see Robson, 2002 for a fuller discussion).

Realists believe in the search for an objective world. However, where they depart from positivists is in recognising that in social research there is always a context that affects this reality. So realists believe that there is a connection between developing tuberculosis (TB) and a particular bacillus. However, whether a person develops TB depends on a range of other factors: these include the quality of housing, the nutritional intake and the person's race (in terms of generational exposure to TB). This classic research done by Bradbury (1933) is used to exemplify realist thinking about research (see Robson, 2002).

A medical example is used to make the case, however when it comes to more social areas the case becomes even stronger. We know, for example, that children who have poor attachment to their parental figures in youth have difficulties in later life forming secure attachment. However, we also know that not all children have these difficulties. Some children have the most appalling attachments in early life and develop into psychologically robust adults. Realists recognise that the outcomes of an action follow from mechanisms acting in particular contexts. In the example the *outcome* (poor relationships in adult life) of an *action* (poor relationships in early childhood) follows from *mechanisms* (the psychological development of the mind) acting in particular *contexts* (how the child was brought up).

Realists believe in experimental evaluation but in a very different way from randomised controlled trials. The logic of the randomised controlled trial is that all variables are controlled (through randomisation of the subjects) apart from one. This variable is then manipulated and resultant change noted. Realist researchers are very critical of this approach (Pawson and Tilley, 1997). The realist is interested in identifying the mechanisms that explain how an action affects outcomes in particular contexts. Experimentation is therefore a very active process. The researcher tries to activate mechanisms to show how there is a pattern of outcomes that relate to various subgroups in the research.

Case Study:
Teaching reading

A new scheme for improving reading is introduced into infant schools in a local authority. The scheme involves parents reading with the child for 10 minutes each night. The local authority would like the scheme to be evaluated.

Traditionally an outcome evaluation would be used for this research. The children's reading progress would be measured and compared with randomly selected children who had not been on the scheme. Process evaluation might also look at how the children and parents made sense of the scheme and why they thought it was successful.

A realist evaluation would look at the evaluation in a different way. It would start from the premise that this scheme (like most services introduced into the real world) would be more effective for some children than for others. What the realist researcher is interested in is why it works for certain children in certain contexts. The researcher's job is to identify the mechanisms that help explain the variability. The mechanisms might be increasing motivation by the teachers, or raising pupils' self-esteem. The mechanisms might be parents' understanding of how to teach reading or of teachers having more time to spend with children reading.

A realist evaluation, instead of trying to control these mechanisms/variables, tries to activate them to see how the pattern of outcomes relates to particular subgroups of people in particular contexts.

Realists believe, like positivists, that there is an external reality. However, they believe that the world is complex and stratified into layers of reality for individuals, groups, organisations and societies. The task of scientific research is to explain this real world through the development of theories. These theories are concerned with how mechanisms explain events. Knowledge and facts are set within a particular time in history. Newton's laws of physics are not facts for ever but simply (by far) the best explanation of the relationship between gravity and mass at a particular point in time. In the same way there are no immutable facts about the best way of treating depressed people, or of teaching reading. Instead there are certain facts about how, for example, cognitive behavioural therapy or a particular type of antidepressant, has the most likely chance of having an effect at this point in our history.

4.5 UNDERTAKING REALIST EVALUATION

Practitioner researchers are likely to see affinities between realist evaluation and the practical issues of undertaking research in their own organisations. In many areas of research randomisation of participants and control of all variables is not only impracticable but also unethical. Realist evaluation is a cyclical research process that allows the practitioner researcher over time to build up a body of evidence about the impact of a service on particular people in particular contexts (Pawson and Tilley, 1997).

Stage 1: The practitioner researcher develops hypotheses about the mechanisms that may affect the outcome of the programme. These hypotheses can be generated in two ways: from a review of the relevant literature, and more importantly from consultation with the various stakeholders. The views of the stakeholders can be gathered by questionnaires, interviews or focus groups. The data are then analysed using some type of qualitative methodology, for example thematic analysis to try to understand what Pawson and Tilley (1997) call the 'folk wisdom' of practitioners. This 'folk wisdom' is about the mechanisms and context that would explain the success of the programme.

Stage 2: The next stage of the research is to see how the mechanisms connect with the programme. There are two pathways for this. The first is when a good deal of data has already been collected. Pawson and Tilley (1997) give the example of re-analysing outcome data from a 20-year prison education programme to see which mechanisms and context best explained the variations in outcome. They were basically trying to understand which of the mechanisms highlighted through the collected folk wisdom made most sense of the data.

The second path is when the programme is in the process of being implemented. In this case the practitioner researcher tries to set up the conditions that they believe will achieve greatest success. The mechanisms that have been generated in Stage 1 are explicitly activated to see if they can increase the programme's effectiveness. In this way the evaluation becomes a real active experiment – similar to action research.

Whichever path is taken, the usual research techniques for data gathering and analysis are used. In a realist evaluation both qualitative and quantitative techniques can be used to measure the success of the programme and to find out more from the stakeholders of why they think it is a success.

Stage 3: The hypotheses about mechanisms that appear most successful are accepted and integrated into the programme. The hypotheses about mechanisms that do not have an effect are rejected. The programme is thus actively changed and modified as it is implemented. Any programme is seen as dynamic rather than static.

In this sense realist evaluation is always formative rather than summative. The purpose of the evaluation is to help develop the effectiveness of a programme by understanding the factors that make it effective. The practitioner researcher needs to have a mechanism – a theory – that explains why the programme has, or does not have, an impact. The evaluation is to test out that theory by gathering data.

Realist evaluations are not simple. They offer the practitioner researcher a model for evaluative research that feels comfortable alongside professional work. In particular the recognition of the differences between people and a rejection of a one-size-fits-all model of service delivery is a helpful way forward.

4.6   THE SHADOW SIDE OF EVALUATION

There is a technical side to evaluation for the practitioner researcher – the use of an outcome or process model, or realist evaluation. There is also the shadow side. The shadow side is concerned with the politics and culture of the organisation. This shadow side is apparent at all stages of evaluation. Evaluation means putting a value on something or making a judgement. It therefore is politically sensitive. There are issues about commissioning, designing and reporting the research.

Commissioning the Research

Though managers may commission research, they do not own it. In addition to the commissioner there are a whole variety of other stakeholders in the research. These stakeholders may be a board of trustees or elected members of a council. Other managers will also be stakeholders. The outcome of the evaluation will affect them too. Then there are the service providers, who are the people who deliver this service. Finally there are the people who are recipients of the service.

What is common about the stakeholders is that they all have a vested interest in the outcomes of the research. However, it is also certain that they will not all have the same interest. So for some it may be chance of promotion, for others the shutting down of a service that they may have invested their life in developing.

The starting point therefore is to acknowledge openly that there are different stakeholders involved with different views. The stakeholders' views can be sought at the beginning of the research. This includes clarifying the scope of the programme's objectives.

In order to address some of the problems the six questions used in the counselling evaluation case study in section 4.3 are a helpful starting place. Drawing a rich picture helps to clarify the shadow aspects.

Designing the Research

Only when the objectives of the programme are clarified is it advisable to move to designing the research. Evaluation covers a number of methods and it is likely that the stakeholders will have different views on what it means. Once again consultation with stakeholders about the design of the evaluation is advisable.

There needs to be clarity about the distinction between an evaluation of outcome or process and the benefits of a realist approach. This may also move the thinking from a bipolar 'it works – it doesn't work' to an 'under what circumstances does some of it work well with some people'. A realist approach will also engage more stakeholders.

Reporting the Research

How the research is reported is crucial. By creating a paper report the researcher is literally bringing the shadow side into the open. This is likely to make a number of stakeholders anxious!

There needs to be clarity, before the research is started, about how it will be reported. At the most pragmatic this is to ensure that there is a realistic time frame. However, practitioner researchers should be aware that good managers are also politically astute. They may well wish to change the time frame if there is an opportunity for the research to have a greater political impact.

It needs to be clarified who will write the research report. Yes – of course the practitioner researcher will! However, what happens if the research findings are not what the commissioner of the research expected. Can he or she rewrite the conclusions, or hide data? (See Chapter 9 for further discussion of a similar scenario.)

Working with the shadow side also means ensuring the stakeholders are aboard for the reporting. Regular briefings about the findings as they develop are one way of ensuring that research cannot be buried. However, the researcher is also part of the shadow side and therefore needs to be as open and transparent as possible.

SUMMARY

- There are many advantages (as well as some disadvantages) for practitioner researchers undertaking research in their own organisation
- The advantages and disadvantages often reside in the shadow side of the organisation

- Practitioner researchers need to be able to work with the shadow side for their research to be valuable to their organisations
- Evaluative research can be about either the outcomes or process of a service. Combining both may be helpful to the practitioner researcher
- Realist evaluation is particularly helpful for practitioner researchers to evaluative the effectiveness of services in their own organisation
- Research is not a neutral activity and working with the shadow side means that research is more likely to make a real difference to people

FURTHER READING

Egan, G. (1994) *Working the Shadow Side*. **San Francisco: Jossey–Bass**

Egan has written extensively on organisation and individual change. In this book he provides a clear explication of the workings of the shadow side of organisations. He does not see the shadow side as negative but simply as another aspect of organisation that needs to be understood. This is a very valuable perspective for the practitioner researcher.

Pawson, R. and Tilley, N. (1997) *Realist Evaluation*. **London: Sage**

This exciting book challenges the traditional ways of evaluation in the social sciences. It provides a clear introduction to the difficulties of evaluating services to people and develops the model of realist evaluation. It may not provide all the answers but it certainly asks all the right questions.

5
Researching Your Own Practice

This chapter is concerned with practitioner researchers' practice as the focus and context of research. The relationship between researcher and research topic is a source of contention within research literature, but for the practitioner researcher this potentially troublesome relationship is central throughout the research. Whilst the practitioner researcher can engage in strategies to clarify roles within the research process, the boundaries between 'practitioner as practitioner' and 'practitioner as researcher' tend to be blurred and unfixed.

The chapter will examine:

- ⇨ The practitioner researcher's intent
- ⇨ Practitioner research
- ⇨ Power in practitioner research

5.1 THE PRACTITIONER RESEARCHER'S INTENT

The practitioner researcher may undertake research with variety of intentions. For example, research may be a requirement of a post, a component of a course of study, career development or personal interest. Before developing the research design the practitioner researcher should be conscious of their intention. The case study below describes potential problems for practitioner researchers who embark upon research without examining and clarifying intent.

Case Study:
Anthony – initiating action research

Anthony is a teacher who has specialised in supporting children with emotional and behavioural difficulties. He works within a small team who receive new referrals and provide input into educational settings on a sessional basis.

Anthony is aware that his local authority advocates a holistic assessment of pupils that examines both their special needs and those needs within a social, family and community context. Current custom and practice within the team is to undertake focused assessment of need relating to the special services provided by the team. This has been the model since the team was established and accorded with professional guidance at the time. The team are satisfied with current practice and believe those who contract their services are also satisfied. Anthony is troubled by this dissonance between professional practice and changes with the conception of assessment by the local authority and decides to 'modernise' the practice of his colleagues and bring it into line with current guidance.

Anthony reviews the literature on research methods and elects to use action research, because of its focus on systematic change within a practice environment. Anthony begins the work with a 'snapshot' of the views of his colleagues through a questionnaire. This is followed by a series of group meetings to discuss and plan for change. He plans to monitor the change and reassess using the same questionnaire at the conclusion of a complete 'action research cycle'.

During the research Anthony meets considerable opposition from colleagues who are both reluctant to engage with the process of action research or address the issues of holistic assessment to which he is trying to draw attention. Anthony feels his colleagues are resistive, intransigent and use outmoded practices.

Anthony's intention is to change practice in a predetermined direction through action research. He perceives change to be of value and necessary; the team hold a contradictory view. Anthony initiates the change process, but he anticipates that the team will implement and maintain the change beyond his involvement. In Chapter 3, the process of change was examined and it was noted that practitioner researchers need to understand their position within the change. Using the grid introduced in Chapter 3 (see Figure 3.1), the outcome of the action research study is likely to be a failure to implement the change.

Anthony's decision to use action research to introduce the change is not an appropriate start point for action research. The practitioner researcher needs to adopt the role of learner and participant rather than controlling the change process. Anthony's view of practice is objectified and simplistic; current practice is wrong and the change he intends to introduce will make it right.

Anthony's perception of change			
		Change actually implemented	
		YES	NO
Change of Value	YES	☺	
	NO		

Team's perception of change			
		Change actually implemented	
		YES	NO
Change of Value	YES		
	NO		☹

FIGURE 5.1 *Perceptions of change*

Practitioner researchers' thinking about their practice is often used implicitly or explicitly to shape research designs, as Anthony's case study demonstrates. Kemmis and McTaggart (2000) identified five different variants by which practice can be perceived (see Box 5.1). These variants demonstrate the perspective of the practitioner researcher and the impact upon the research design. Anthony's perspective of practice and research intent is that the team can be studied objectively as a group, the second variant.

Box 5.1   Variants of practice

- Practice as individual behaviour, to be studied objectively
- Practice as group behaviour or ritual, to be studied objectively
- Practice as individual action, to be studied from the perspective of the subjective
- Practice as social action or tradition, to be understood from the perspective of the subjective
- Practice as reflexive, to be studied dialectically

(Kemmis and McTaggart, 2000)

Practitioner researchers adopt a view of the world based on their own assumptions about the world. In the case study, Anthony assumes the model of assessment promoted by his professional body is correct and should be adopted. Practitioner researchers should adopt a critical stance towards such assertions about practice by asking the question recommended in Chapter 1:

What is the evidence that underpins this initiative?

Practitioner research is a significant and legitimate form of social change (McNiff, 2002). In order to recognise this, practitioner researchers need to understand the subject, the context and the implications of the change before commencing research. This will enable them to adopt a stance towards the research that is:

- Critical, not built upon the assumption that there is a single 'truth' about practice. There may be many 'truths' held by individual practitioners and shared within groups
- Neutral, not presenting change as a *fait accompli* to practitioners. The practitioner researcher has no organisational authority to implement change, practitioners will neither engage nor follow through the change unless the practitioner researcher is perceived as trustworthy and agenda-less

A helpful starting point for practitioner research is not to use action research to facilitate change in others. Instead practitioners can use action research to facilitate change in themselves. This is known as practitioner research.

5.2 PRACTITIONER RESEARCH

This section will examine the development of practitioner research as an aspect of action research. Action research, as has been shown in Chapter 3, is a composite term for several designs focusing on action leading to change. The burgeoning interest in action research by practitioners intimates dissatisfaction with more traditional approaches to research where researcher, researched and context are regarded discretely. The practitioner in practitioner research is an integral part of the research process and outcomes feed immediately into local practice.

The involvement of practitioners, from education, health and social care, in research and audit is recognised as a component of professional practice. There are, however, many levels of involvement and practitioners may perceive themselves to be only the end users of research, rather than taking an active role in the construction of knowledge through research about their own practice. Consequently, the potential for the development of knowledge by practitioners is not exploited (Eraut, 1994).

The outcomes of research carried out by external or academic researchers within practice are not integrated into the real world of practice as understood by those within that environment. Validity is not defined by objective criteria laid down by researchers and academics; it is a matter for the reflective users of the research (Freshwater and Rolfe, 2001). Practitioner researchers might ask external researchers who wish them to be research participants some questions about how knowledge is being constructed from the research. They should enquire for whom knowledge is being constructed, whose knowledge is seen as the most important and who is best placed to construct this knowledge (Deshler and Grudens-Schuck, 2000). Practitioner researchers should ensure that research directly benefits practice and is constructed by people who understand the field. Practitioner research presents the opportunity for practitioners to develop research that is meaningful and applicable.

Case Study:
Simon – doing practitioner research

Simon is a charge nurse and a practitioner researcher working in a mental health day care service. He wishes to undertake a small-scale investigation into the delivery of a therapeutic group, which he facilitates.

☐ What problems may Simon encounter with seeking approval for this research?

☐ What problems may Simon encounter in carrying out this research?

☐ What ethical dilemmas are posed by Simon's research?

Simon is both researcher and practitioner and these roles are not discrete. It would be difficult for Simon, his colleagues and service users with whom he works to determine when Simon is acting as a researcher and when he is acting as a practitioner. In traditional modes of research such role blurring would almost certainly present overwhelming problems in carrying out the research. Practitioner research challenges such conventional thinking about research. In doing so an extensive field of research is opened up for practitioners within the workplace. To a point, practitioners have always engaged in systematic approaches to problem solving and practitioner research is little different: 'Practice and practitioner research may mutually benefit from considering how far the perspectives and methods of one provide a template for the other' (Shaw, 2002: 9).

Practitioner research enables professionals, like Simon, to explore practice in a systematic, but not dissociated, manner. It recognises that rather than attempting to eliminate researcher effects, the research should, through the use of reflexivity, acknowledge these effects and integrate them into the design. This research challenges conventional thinking about the field and the practitioner researcher is forced to ask questions about the values embedded in his or her thinking (Dadds, 2006).

Chapter 3 has already introduced action research and differentiated between action research, participatory action research and emancipatory action research. Practitioner research is a fourth form of action research. It is research carried out by practitioners for the purpose of advancing their own practice (McLeod, 1999). It is a strategy by which practitioners can use research to assist them to reflect in a systematic manner and learn from their own practice. However, there is 'no sacrosanct way of conducting practitioner research' (Dadds, 2006: 2).

There are a variety of methods adopted by practitioners, all of which share an action orientation and a practice focus. Furlong and Oancea (2005) have attempted to describe the range of methods in the form of a research continuum:

> applied and practice based research – an area situated between academic-led theoretical pursuits . . . and research informed practice and consisting of a multitude of models of research explicitly conducted in, with, and/or for practice. (Furlong and Oancea, 2005: 9).

Rearick and Feldman (1999) undertook an analysis of action research in educational settings. Through this analysis they defined some of the parameters of action research as it was practised. The themes covered the 'product' of the research, the 'mode of reflection' and the 'orientation'. By plotting these themes Rearick and Feldman created what they described as an action research space. This space provides a liberating 'action research arena' rather than constraining 'action research definition'.

One of the studies reported in Rearick and Feldman's (1999) paper is by Hollingsworth (1994). The approach Hollingsworth describes is a collaborative venture between teachers and the author. Hollingsworth engaged teachers in conversation about their work over a period of time. These conversations created the space for both longitudinal research and a means of supporting teachers and those learning to teach. The teachers in the study learned about their work through sharing their own biographies and through interaction and conversation. Hollingsworth described the research method as being based within the conversations. These conversations enabled participants to clarify and reformulate ideas within a group in order to develop a shared understanding and a common story. Through the research process teachers gained an understanding of classroom relationships, diversity of values and increased critical awareness of power relationships inside the school.

Rearick and Feldman's (1999) analysis of Hollingsworth's paper suggests that the area within the action research space is defined by:

- A product that is personal – each participant, by engaging with the research, undergoes a personal learning experience about his or her own learning
- A mode of reflection that is collaborative/autobiographical – reflection is both highly personal and shared as a group in a collaborative venture
- An orientation that is emancipatory – through a systematic and sustained examining of learning about learning, participants developed an awareness of the impact of assumptions and social structures on their learning behaviour

Qualitative research is a rigorous and systematic process, and Hollingsworth's approach appears, on the surface, to debunk rigour in favour of conversation. However, her method is underpinned by reflexivity, an essential component of action research. Reflexivity recognises that there is a continuous exchange between the researcher, the researched and the research, which is fundamental to the action research process. As such reflexivity should be incorporated into the research in a systematic and rigorous manner.

Case Study:
Simon – doing practitioner research (option 1)

Simon proposes that the context of the research will be a comparison of two six-week therapeutic groups. In the first group Simon acts as group leader and in the second he acts as group facilitator. The intention of the research is to:

- Analyse the processes at work within the group
- Ascertain whether the group is attaining its outcomes
- Improve the quality of the group through reflection on practice

The literature reports that both styles of leadership are appropriate for the particular group, but Simon is unsure which style he is personally more able to deliver. During the groups, Simon collects data in the form of:

- Detailed observations of the group
- Audio recordings of group sessions
- Feedback at the mid-and end-points of each of the groups about the perceived qualities and preferences for each group
- Personal reflection

(Continued)

(Continued)

The area within the action research space (Rearick and Feldman, 1999) in which Simon is working can be described as follows:

- The product of the research is professional. The purpose of doing the research is to enable Simon to improve his group work skills. This contributes to his professional development as a nurse
- The mode of reflection of the research is collaborative. Simon requires the perspectives of the group members in order to assess the quality of his group work skills subjectively and objectively
- The orientation is practical. Since the purpose of the research is to examine group work it requires a practical orientation that will enable Simon to draw out interaction and the making of meaning by the group

Practitioner research also uses 'cases' that give practitioners the opportunity to tell stories about practice and use them as the basis of learning. However, not all stories are 'cases'. To call something a 'case' is to make a theoretical claim that it is a 'case of something' or an instance of a larger class (Shulman, 2002). Cases are candid, dramatic, highly readable accounts of events or a series of events from practice (McGinnis, 2001). Practitioner research, in this form, consists of reflecting upon and re-working intellectually, core professional experiences (Dadds, 2006); in this way it can be seen as phenomenological knowledge. There is increasing interest in the documentation and systematic analysis of practitioner stories or narratives (Ghaye and Lillyman, 2000a; Ghaye et al., 2000; Greenhalgh and Hurwitz, 1998).

Practitioners engage in informal research throughout their careers. When presented with a problem, practitioners draw upon various forms of existing and new knowledge in order to resolve the problem through action. There is, therefore, a close relationship between professional development and practitioner research. This is exemplified in regulatory bodies in the UK, such as the Nursing and Midwifery Council and the Health Professions Council, which require practitioners to complete portfolios of professional development evidence before being permitted to continue practising. The portfolio, when undertaken using a systematic reflective approach, is itself a form of action research. A further term identified as a component of practitioner research is self-study. This can be linked to the use of reflection in the practice setting. A natural affinity exists between action research and reflection (Ghaye and Lillyman, 2000b). The use of self-study demonstrates how reflection is used within an action research framework (Lomax et al., 1996; Richards, 1996).

Case Study:
Simon – doing practitioner research (option 2)

Simon proposes that the context of the research will be the therapeutic groups that he facilitates. The intention of the research is to:

- Analyse the process of reflection in action within the group
- Understand how critical reflection is developed
- Improve the quality of the group through reflecting on practice

Simon is aware that, as a skilled group worker, he uses reflection in action. However, it is something he also recognises he does not use in a systematic way. In order to better understand this process he uses a group that he facilitates as a context, and a data collection strategy that includes:

- Retrospective observations of the use of reflection in action
- Feedback from the group about the use of reflection in action
- Audio recordings of group session
- Personal reflection

The area within the action research space (Rearick and Feldman, 1999) in which Simon is working can be described as follows:

- The product of the research is personal. The purpose of doing the research is to enable Simon to better understand his own learning style
- The mode of reflection of the research is autobiographical. Simon's interest is in his own learning and, therefore, it is autobiographical
- The orientation is technical. Simon is seeking to improve the way he learns in practice

---

The dilemma posed by practitioner research is whether the practitioner is engaging in research or practice. This question implicitly asks whether practitioner research is research at all. Rearick and Feldman's (1999) work on the action research space offers a creative way of thinking about practitioner research. It does not address how quality should be assessed. Furlong and Oancea (2005) suggest that there are four dimensions of quality: (1) epistemic, (2) technological, (3) capacity building and value for people and (4) economic, each of which are subdivided. They propose this as a point from which to start, rather than a definitive answer. In doing so, the practitioner researcher has a method for evaluating and defending the quality of his or her own practitioner research to others. This will help practitioner research to be seen by the entire research community as valid research that makes a significant contribution to the work of public services.

In the case study Simon's practitioner research highlighted a number of issues. The relatively recent development of practitioner research has meant that there is limited reliable information about how reflexivity between the researcher and the research can be managed. Fraser's (1997) study identifies some of the issues that may emerge within either of Simon's studies.

- Personal values and potential for bias. Both of Simon's research projects may be perceived as biased. An external reviewer may suggest that he has a vested interest in attaining positive outcomes. Simon may also be committed to working in a particular way, and be unlikely to perceive alternative ways of working that might be more effective.
- The researcher's role within the organisation. Simon's intention may be to disregard his role within the organisation and focus on open and honest communication with all participants. If this is achieved, it may continue to be problematic for participants to see Simon in anything other than a position of power as, for example: 'group facilitator' or 'senior nurse'.
- Confidentiality and anonymity. Simon's research is being done at a local level and maintaining anonymity and confidentiality could become impossible.
- Role conflict issues. Simon, as a practitioner within the organisation, is both a therapist and a researcher. This dual role may be problematic to him, his colleagues and service users with whom he works. This has the potential to cause harm both to the research and to the therapist role.
- Time constraints: with the blurring of barriers between research and practice Simon may experience problems in identifying time to fulfil either component of his role. This is a particular problem with action research, which is developmental and cannot be placed within a rigid research protocol.

The problems highlighted by Fraser (1997) are the practical problems that practitioner researchers will encounter when embarking on a study. Practitioner research must be sold to managers, colleagues, academics and governance and ethics committees. Box 5.2 brings together some strategies for undertaking practitioner research.

Box 5.2   Strategies for managing practitioner research

Have confidence in the design

The practitioner researcher needs to regularly revisit the purpose of the study and the reasons for selecting a practitioner research design.

Acknowledge difference

Practitioner research is the subject of considerable scepticism from academics and other researchers. It is a relatively new and developing field of research

(Continued)

(Continued)

that challenges traditional beliefs about the nature of knowledge and knowledge construction and, inevitably, creates tensions. World-views cannot be challenged in the simple terms of 'rights and wrongs'; practitioner researchers need to develop skills in arguing for and defending their position.

Lead the way

The greater the quality and quantity of practitioner research that is put in the public domain, the easier it will be for others to follow. Undertaking practitioner research will strengthen the professional aspiration of making a significant contribution to improving the standard of service for service users. This is also bi-directional; new practitioner researchers need to familiarise themselves with the growing practitioner research literature.

Stay focused

The strength of practitioner research lies in the focus of the project. Practitioner researchers should focus their attention on the immediate environment and its relationship to the research question.

Be aware of scale

Practitioner research is by definition local and small-scale. Practitioner researchers need to be clear not just about what they can achieve, but the significance of the achievement to the environment in which the study is occurring.

Build relationships

Practitioner research relies on collaborative working with colleagues, service users and managers amongst others at various points within the study. By building and maintaining these relationships the practitioner researcher develops the bedrock on which he or she can develop the study.

Communicate clearly

Practitioner research presents many ethical dilemmas to be resolved before and during the study. Communicating intent and potential hazards enables study participants to make informed judgements about whether they wish to continue.

Be reflective and reflexive

Practitioner research cannot be removed from the practitioner researcher. The relationship between the person and the study, therefore, is part of the study. Developing the skill to manage this relationship is not trivial; it is an imperative and should not be regarded lightly.

Create change

Practitioner research is about creating a positive force for change in the environment of the study. When change ceases the practitioner researcher should examine why and take action.

(Continued)

(Continued)

Be sensitive to power and politics

Practitioner researchers need to be sensitive to subtle changes to the power and politics that exist within the environment of study. These changes may present significant hurdles to be surmounted; equally the shift may be a positive change that can be harnessed within the study.

Get support

Practitioner researchers should not be undertaking work in isolation. The importance of negotiating supervision and ensuring that it is accessed is fundamental to the successful completion of research.

(With acknowledgement to: Fraser, 1997; McNiff, 2002; Robson, 2002; Shaw, 2002; Dadds, 2006)

Practitioner research has not advanced in parallel throughout the public services. The documented work on practitioner research in education is considerably greater than in health and social care. This may relate to prominence of experimental research and the perception of the randomised controlled trial as the 'gold standard' of research in health and social care. It may also relate to the extensive and bureaucratic structures that exist within health and social care that are influenced by the NHS hierarchy of evidence. Such structures are slow to evolve; they take time to accept that alternative research worlds exist and research carried out in unusual and creative ways is not automatically 'bad research'.

Practitioner research presents practitioner researchers with a new vista of research. The methods can be developed and applied within a range of practice settings and will generate knowledge, promote reflective learning and change in local practices. Action research methods, including practitioner research, are gaining greater acceptance alongside traditional methods of research. It is only through undertaking and publishing good quality studies that the method will be strengthened. Strengthening should not be read as making rigid a set of techniques (McNiff, 2002). Rather, as a means of filling Rearick and Feldman's (1999) 'action research space' with a variety of innovative methods that share the goals of action research.

In traditional research methods there is usually an end point, a goal. However, in practitioner research the process of constructing knowledge can be better than the knowledge that is produced, no matter how useful the outcomes (Deshler and Grudens-Schuck, 2000). Change occurs in the field from the point when practitioners begin thinking about research:

Practitioner research is a challenging and exacting undertaking. It demands open-mindedness, courage in the face of self-critique and public sharing, emotional fortitude in dealing with uncertainty and profound change, spiritual energy in sustaining curiosity, compassion and the eternal search for new, improved practices. (Dadds, 2006: 9)

We have spent some time discussing practitioner research as a particular method within the overarching framework of action research. As Chapter 1 argues, all research worlds are available to practitioners and methods should be selected primarily on congruency with the purpose of the research. Practitioner research is broadly consistent with the practitioner's focus on change, collaboration and reflection. Practitioner research offers the opportunity to develop new and creative approaches to resolving the messy problems of practice drawing upon a research design that is not imposed on practice, but integrates with practice.

5.3 POWER IN PRACTITIONER RESEARCH

In the previous section we examined some of the strategies required for managing practitioner research. Essentially these are all about the practitioner researcher gaining power.

The research process is permeated with relations and influence based on power. Practitioner researchers need first to be aware of where and when power is being exercised, and, secondly, to be aware of their own power in order for it to be used effectively and with the minimum damage to others. Two distinct sources of power can be identified:

- Power within the research process
- Power within the research outcomes

Power within the Research Process

Power within the research process is visible in different forms. The practitioner researcher has access to, and uses, power in many of these forms. As expert practitioners, practitioner researchers possess power that can be transferred to the research. The practitioner researcher also generates power that can be used in future research by undertaking research. This relationship can be seen in Figure 5.2.

Expert practitioners bring resource, expert and position power to the role of practitioner researcher (Handy, 1988). An experienced teacher knows how to teach, but also has experience of, for example:

- The management of education at a local and national level
- Accessing managers and budget holders

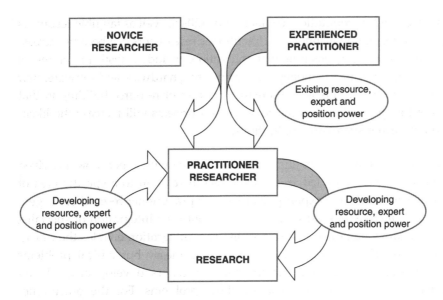

FIGURE 5.2 *The power cycle of the practitioner researcher*

- Making an informed and reliable case for additional resources
- Engaging the support of powerful stakeholders
- Creating a focus of attention by stakeholders and those with additional power in relation to specific projects

However, power cannot automatically be transferred from the role of the practitioner to the practitioner researcher. Being an expert practitioner and an expert researcher are not synonymous. Practitioner researchers, therefore, need to be adept at maximising the transferability of power and developing power within their new role.

Resource power The expert practitioner may possess considerable resource power within the organisation. This power may have been accrued over years of practice through the demonstrated efficient management of resources. When the practitioner adopts the role of practitioner researcher these skills can be transferred at both a practical level and through the confidence of resource holders within the organisation.

Practitioner researchers can attain greater resource power through their research activities. The practitioner researcher's knowledge of the systems for research and research governance will enable them to know about and access resources outside their own organisation. Through meticulous completion of research funding applications practitioner researchers can begin to build resources over which they have control. This may include virtual resources such as reputation, contacts and skills as well as tangible resources such as information technology. Practitioner researchers can become increasingly autonomous by ensuring that applications include realistic requirements in terms of, for example: money, time, computing hardware and software, staff replacement costs. This is a cumulative process of resource building in that successful applications leading to successful projects will increase the likelihood of further successful applications.

Expert power   Practitioners often come to research with expert power derived from recognised knowledge and expertise in relation to a specific area of practice. Similarly, the expert power held by practitioner researchers is generally distinctive and individually unique with the integration of specialist practice knowledge and research skills. This integration enables the practitioner researcher to perceive and frame the messy but critical problems of practice. Once framed, practitioner researchers develop original and systematic approaches to resolving these problems. For the practitioner researcher expertise in the delivery of good quality research also provides the basis for expert power, through knowledge and application of good research governance.

Position power   Position power is identified as being part of a valid information stream, the right of access to networks and the right to organise work (Handy, 1988). The expert practitioner may have developed reliable and resilient networks over time. Such networks, and the skills associated with maintaining them, are similar to those required by the practitioner researcher. For the practitioner researcher, position power is concerned with knowing and understanding research designs and the procedures for completion of trustworthy research.

The practitioner researcher's position power is underwritten by the organisation. Organisations may not be consistent about the need for practitioner researchers and, as such, practitioner researchers may not be able to develop a consistent and substantial portfolio of work. In order to demonstrate the 'added value' of active practitioner researchers within an organisation, practitioner researchers need to disseminate their work as widely as possible. Many practitioners have a broad network of peers with whom they network and share good practice. Practitioner researchers need to adopt similar tactics to assert their position power within the organisation.

Power within the Outcomes of Research

The outcomes of research create and shape a world-view, which empowers some and disempowers others. The primary impact of the outcomes is on the organisation, the practitioner researcher and the end user. The end user of research might be the patient, the pupil or the client. This group have traditionally been excluded from most aspects of research; however Chapter 8 indicates how this position has shifted in recent years. The following three examples, each starting from the same scenario, give some indication of the relationship between research outcomes and power.

Case Study:
Sheila – power and the outcomes of research

Sheila was commissioned by her employer to undertake research to measure the uptake of a 'drop-in advice and support' service for clients with substance misuse problems. The findings of the study indicated that uptake was poor throughout the week and did not justify the necessary investment of time and resources.

Sheila framed the issue in very simple terms, as one of attendance of service users at the drop-in. The research, therefore, encouraged the perception of a problem in which the Trust provided a service and service users did not use the service. This perception is disempowering of a service user group who are already socially excluded and often vulnerable. Sheila's employer, a financially constrained NHS Trust, was delighted with the research. The Trust removed the drop-in service and was able to use the saving to reduce its budget deficit. The Trust argued that it had tried to provide a service, but research had shown that this client group did not require this service.

The outcome of the study empowered the organisation. The Trust used the research findings to justify a cut in the services it provided to service users. In empowering the Trust the outcomes disempowered service users. Sheila's power as a practitioner researcher within the Trust increased.

Case Study:
Karen – power and the outcomes of research

Karen undertook research within a health care setting in which she explored the use of a 'drop-in advice and support' service for clients with substance misuse problems. The findings of the study indicated that many of the clients of the service did not use the drop-in because they were unable to get to the service during 10.00 and 16.00 when it was open. Clients wanted a service that was open between 16.00 and 20.00 during the week. As a consequence the Trust changed the times the service was open.

Karen framed the issue in terms of opening times and access to the drop-in service. The power invested in the research and the associated outcomes was

(Continued)

(Continued)

within the control of the researcher and the Trust. The Trust reluctantly agreed to support the findings and change service provision. There was an improvement of services for service users, but uptake remained poor. The outcomes had not empowered the clients because they were not stakeholders in the research. With continued poor uptake the Trust felt that it had invested further into a service, at a time of cash restraint, but the service remained poorly used. Karen experienced a loss of power, through being implicitly blamed by the Trust for carrying out research that had not benefited either the Trust or service users.

Case Study:
Annalisa – power and the outcomes of research

Annalisa undertook research within a health care setting in which she explored the use of a 'drop-in advice and support' service for clients with substance misuse problems. The study adopted an action research design where Annalisa explored the service with all the stakeholders, service users, the Trust and colleagues in the substance misuse service. The outcome of the research suggested that the drop-in was not the model of choice and that the service should move to an out-of-hours appointment-based service.

Annalisa framed the issue as one of service provision and had incorporated all the stakeholders into the development of the study. The Trust agreed to fund the service development and uptake increased significantly. Service users were empowered through the study because they had contributed their views that had been incorporated into the outcomes. The Trust had been empowered because it could demonstrate provision of a cost-effective, research-based service for which there was good uptake. Annalisa was empowered because the research was designed not to disempower any stakeholders and received approbation from both Trust and service users.

The distribution of power in research outcomes is often unequal. Empowerment of one group of stakeholders often leads to disempowerment of others. The practitioner researcher should be conscious of the power in the research process and determine how best the research can be carried out maintaining good quality research that does not intentionally disempower any group of stakeholders.

Power conflicts within research

Practitioners within public sector organisations in the UK, in particular the National Health Service, are increasingly burdened by a bureaucratic system of research governance that is impacting upon research as it is practised in the field and this is discussed in the following chapter. Whilst recognising the importance of governance systems to prevent bad practice, there has been an unintended restriction on innovation and the legitimate development of knowledge through research. The three key structures in the NHS are the hierarchy of knowledge, where the randomised controlled trial is seen as the 'gold standard', the research governance structures and the ethical appraisal systems, both of which are populated by members whose perception of research is in accord with the NHS hierarchy. A more detailed consideration of these structures is featured in Chapter 6.

These governance structures are a source of power and control. Whilst it is noted that structures are becoming less dominated by a traditional view of objective world research, there remains a strong adherence to traditional modes of research. Those with knowledge tend to assume positions of power and those with power define and regulate what counts as valid knowledge in a self-perpetuating cycle (Freshwater and Rolfe, 2001).

When dealing with research governance practitioner researchers should be aware when their research is being downgraded in relation to research that is rated more highly within the NHS hierarchy of evidence. If power is being exerted in this way then practitioner researchers should challenge this by asking whose knowledge counts. Expert power is also about defence of a position; anyone who has been through a *viva voce* will be familiar with this process. Practitioner researchers do not defend their findings in isolation, they must defend the systematic method used that led to the findings; and which demonstrates the strength of the research. Whether or not the findings are palatable to the organisation is irrelevant if the method can be demonstrated to be trustworthy.

The reliance in public sector organisations on a hierarchy of evidence in which the randomised controlled trial is perceived as the ideal, presents some problems in the defence of method. Practitioner researchers may find themselves defending a small-scale qualitative study where the preferred approach is large-scale experimental study. Mounting a robust defence in such circumstances may be difficult and challenging. It is at this point that practitioner researchers trust their own research skills and chosen method. Research using appropriate methods, undertaken by practitioners, can present an accurate picture of practice and practitioner researchers are in a good position to do this.

SUMMARY

- There is a link between practitioner research and professional development that presents an opportunity to develop and strengthen systematic thinking within practice

- The action research space is a defined area in which practitioner researchers can locate and develop innovative research designs
- Practitioner research that emphasises change, reflection and collaboration can offer a shared sense of identity to practitioner researchers
- Action research, including practitioner research, presents novel problems for which there are no tested responses. There are several strategies by which practitioners can equip themselves to deal with potential problems
- Power is inherent within the research process. The practitioner comes to research with some power and can develop that resource through practitioner research. Awareness of where and when power is being used, both positively and negatively, is essential for the practitioner researcher
- The problems of practice cannot be universally addressed through the systematic application of evidence-based practice. Practitioners require tools by which practice problems can be researched in a manner congruent to the environment of practice

FURTHER READING

Furlong, J. and Oancea, A. (2005) *Assessing Quality in Applied and Practice Based Educational Research – a Framework for Discussion.* **Oxford: Oxford University Department of Education**

This discussion paper outlines the issues and difficulties of integrating practice-based research into the mainstream research community. It provides a framework for defining practice-based research and assessing its quality.

McNiff, J. (2002) *Action Research: Principles and Practice.* **2nd edition. London: Routledge Falmer**

McNiff outlines the principles and practice of action research in an accessible manner. The book contains reflective chapters written by those involved in action research, which give the work a sense of practical reality.

6
Undertaking Ethical Research

All research has to be ethical and comply with appropriate ethical regulations. Doing ethical research and obtaining ethical approval to do research are not synonymous. This chapter will explore ethical issues relating to research as well as the local and national structures that researchers have to engage with in order to undertake research. In particular it will focus on:

⇨ Organisational structures
⇨ Professional guidelines and regulations
⇨ Doing ethical research
⇨ Obtaining ethical approval
⇨ Striking a balance between bureaucracy and ethical research

6.1 THE ORGANISATIONAL STRUCTURES

Jumping through Hoops to Gain Approval to Conduct Research

Practitioner researchers need to jump through a number of hoops before the research can start. Approval may be required from any or all of the individuals and institutions listed in Box 6.1.

Box 6.1   Individuals and institutions involved in the approval process

- Line manager
- Senior management of the organisation
- Research supervisor
- Local gatekeepers to get access to research participants
- Local Research and Development (R&D) Committees
- Research Ethics Committees (RECs)

The number of hoops to be jumped through varies considerably depending on the research site and the nature of the research. At one end of the spectrum is the independently funded researcher doing participant observation research in a voluntary organisation. Other than seeking the approval of the organisation, there may be no further hoops to negotiate before starting the research.

At the other end of the spectrum is the NHS-employed researcher who wants to use NHS patients as research participants. They are likely to need the formal approval of all the individuals and institutions listed in Box 6.1 and this often requires time, effort and a great deal of perseverance.

There is a consensus that NHS researchers currently have to jump through more hoops than other practitioner researchers. As a result, much of this chapter draws upon examples related to NHS research.

Case Study:
An example of too much bureaucracy in research

Researchers were asked to evaluate a new method of health delivery which had been introduced county-wide. The research was small scale with funding spread over 12 months to support a research officer for six months, occasional travel, as well as consumables (stationery, phone calls, tapes etc.). The research involved self-completion questionnaires sent to a range of health care staff, interviews with a subset of these health care workers and focus groups with service users receiving the new service.

Approval for the study was obtained from a university Ethics Committee to obtain sponsorship. Applications were then made to a Strategic Health Authority for honorary contracts for the researchers in order to progress the application for REC approval. Following the collation of these documents, a formal submission

(Continued)

(Continued)

was made to the REC. The REC requested a number of minor amendments and the study was approved one month later.

Approval from the REC represented only the first part of the administrative process. Formal application then had to be made to the Research and Development (R&D) Groups of each Trust that covered the local area. This included 13 Primary Care Trusts, five Acute Trusts, and two Mental Health Trusts. Not surprisingly, the administrative load was extremely time-consuming, and an enormous volume of (often duplicated) paperwork was generated (see Figure 6.1). Moreover, each Trust had its own individual R&D procedures, thereby complicating the process still further.

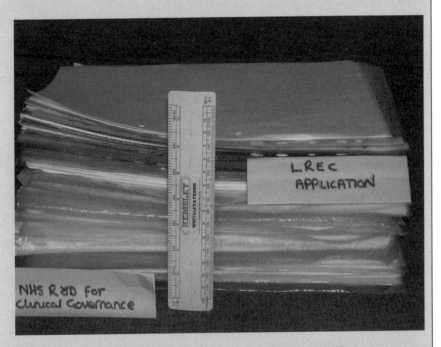

FIGURE 6.1 *Can such a large amount of paperwork be justified for this project?*

The whole process of obtaining approval took over six months to complete and the great majority of the salaried time of the paid researcher. In retrospect the project should have requested more funding to allow for this. Since this project took place the organisation of research governance in this county has been 'streamlined' and is no longer so onerous.

Research Ethics Committees

Until the late twentieth century much research was unregulated and as a result malpractice in research went unchecked. It was, for example, not uncommon for research participants to be unaware that they were taking part in research and the collection of signed consent forms from research participants was not always routine.

In the current climate the situation is rather different as a result of greater service user involvement, risk management, increased litigation and a more defensive approach to practice as people feel the need to protect themselves. There are now a number of checks in all care systems to ensure that research is conducted ethically and protect the rights, safety and dignity of research participants as well as the researcher.

In the health field this is presided over by the Central Office of Research Ethics Committees (see www.corec.org.uk/). The Central Office for Research Ethics Committees (COREC), working on behalf of the Department of Health in England, coordinates the development of operational systems for local and multi-centre Research Ethics Committees (RECs). COREC in England works closely with colleagues with similar responsibilities in Northern Ireland, Scotland and Wales.

COREC has produced a standard ethics application form so that researchers only have to fill in one form even if they have to apply to more than one REC. The form, however, is lengthy and daunting to a novice researcher. It requires supporting letters from the research sponsor, an independent peer review, details of indemnity arrangements for both negligent and non-negligent harm and a number of signatures (e.g. of research gatekeepers, managers, supervisors). A large number of hard copies of the form (up to 20) have to be sent to the REC as well as the electronic version. Researchers are generally asked to attend the committee meeting at which their research is discussed. It is normal for changes to be requested, quite often of sufficient size to require a further formal submission. Practitioner researchers linked to a higher education institute may also have to apply for approval from a university Ethics Committee. The process of obtaining approval thus requires large amounts of patience, resources and time.

Research Governance: a Belts and Braces Approach

The need for this type of rigorous and systematic monitoring of research was made apparent by the relatively recent case at 'Alder Hey' (see Redfern, 2000). Dick van Velzen, a pathologist working at the Alder Hey Children's hospital in Liverpool, ordered the removal of organs from dead infants' bodies for research purposes, without relatives' consent. Consent was either not obtained at all or consent forms were signed but without the relatives' fully understanding what was involved. The parents of those whose organs were retained had not agreed to the long-term retention of the organs, and sometimes only became aware of this many years after their child had been buried or cremated. This led to a public inquiry – The Royal Liverpool Children's Inquiry (Redfern, 2000) – and prompted the development of systems to ensure that this type of incident would not happen again.

The Research Governance Framework (RGF) is designed to improve research quality and safeguard the public (see Box 6.2). Full details may be found on the RGF website www.dh.gov.uk//. The framework was originally applied in healthcare settings but has now been rolled out to social care organisations. The aims of the Research Governance Framework are:

- Enhancing ethical and scientific quality
- Promoting good practice
- Reducing adverse incidents and ensuring lessons are learned from them
- Preventing poor performance and misconduct

There is a certain degree of overlap between the RGF and RECs, notably the requirement of both to enhance the ethical quality of research. This is a source of confusion.

Box 6.2   The Research Governance Framework

Under the RGF, health and social care organisations have a legal requirement to ensure compliance with standards in a number of domains. This has resulted in the development of a large number of systems and a huge bureaucracy to ensure that all research adheres to these standards in the following domains:

- Safeguarding health and safety of researchers and research participants
- Ensuring financial probity, including access to systems for costing and financial management of research
- Documenting agreements with research partners to allocate responsibilities
- Ensuring all staff are aware of the RGF
- Gaining approval of research by both trusts and RECs and making arrangements to ensure that the approved protocols are being adhered to
- Recording any adverse events
- Making compliance with the RGF a term of all relevant employment contracts
- Arranging for NHS honorary contracts to be issued to non-NHS researchers
- Ensuring all research has a nominated sponsor

(Continued)

(Continued)

- Ensuring all research is subject to independent expert review through accepted scientific and professional channels
- Detection of and a system for dealing with research misconduct and fraud
- Involving consumers in the development and execution of research projects
- Insuring all research is appropriately disseminated
- Putting systems in place for the identification of research-based intellectual property
- Ensuring access to systems, where appropriate, for ownership, exploitation and income from intellectual property

The list is lengthy and the task for practitioner researchers of meeting all the many exacting standards is onerous, particularly for the self-funded researcher conducting a small project. It is often a source of deep frustration for practitioner researchers who complain that they spend more time and resources meeting the RGF standards than actually doing the research (Department of Health, 2005a). The final section in this chapter (section 6.5) addresses these concerns and asks whether the bureaucracy has gone too far.

6.2   PROFESSIONAL GUIDELINES AND REGULATIONS

The process of obtaining approval to conduct research is seen by many practitioner researchers as unnecessarily bureaucratic. Many argue that they are by definition bound by their own professional code of ethics and that therefore much of the lengthy bureaucracy is superfluous, particularly that which is conflicting and repetitive. Professional guidance is not always sufficient as it failed to work in the case of van Velzen at Alder Hey. There are, however, numerous guidelines for conducting research produced by professional groups as well as for professional academic associations and research councils and these are very useful (see Boxes 6.3 and 6.4).

Box 6.3   Holders of professional guidelines and ethical codes of practice

- Professional groups, such as the Chartered Society of Physiotherapists or the Royal College of Nursing
- Professional academic associations such as the British Sociological Association or the British Psychological Society
- Research councils such as the Medical Research Council and Economic and Social Research Council

Do you know who holds the ethical code of practice for your profession?

We would strongly advise each practitioner researcher to look towards guidelines relating to their profession to support their research practice. There are a number of sites to assist the practitioner researcher. A list of useful sites is set out in Box 6.4.

Box 6.4   Useful websites

Biotechnology and Biological Sciences Research Council (BBSRC)	www.bbsrc.ac.uk
British Psychological Association	www.bps.org.uk/index.cfm
British Sociological Association	www.britsoc.co.uk
Bulletin of Medical Ethics	www.bullmedeth.info
The Chartered Society for Physiotherapists	www.csp.org.uk
Economic and Social Research Council	www.esrc.ac.uk
Engineering and Physical Sciences Research Council (EPSRC)	www.epsrc.ac.uk/website/index.aspx
Good Research Practice Guidelines (issued in 2000)	www.mrc.ac.uk/pdf-good research practice. pdf
Health and Safety Executive (HSE)	www.hse.gov.uk/hsehome.htm
MRC-published guidance on the Ethical Conduct of Research on the Mentally Incapacitated	www.mrc.ac.uk/pdf-ethics-mental.pdf
Multi-Centre Research Ethics Committee	www.corec.org.uk/
Nuffield Council on Bioethics	www.nuffieldbioethics.org/home/
Royal College of Nursing Research and Development Coordinating Centre	www.man.ac.uk/rcn/
Safeguarding Good Scientific Practice	www.ost.gov.uk/research/councils/safe.htm
Social Services Research Group	www.ssrg.org.uk
Research Ethics Resources on WWW	www.ethicsweb.ca/resources

All websites accessed 21 February 2006

These sites include statements of ethical practice or guidelines pertaining to research to encourage practitioners and other professionals to take responsibility for their own ethical research practice. The types of areas that are covered are:

- Professional integrity
- Relations with, and obligations to, sponsors and funders
- Relationships with research participants
- Responsibilities toward research participants
- Anonymity, privacy and confidentiality
- Covert research (that which is done without the knowledge of research participants)

Professional integrity relates to the responsibility of researchers to safeguard the interests of those involved in their research and to report their findings accurately. This can create conflicts of interest, as illustrated in the following case study.

Case Study:
An example of conflicting interests

Jim, a practitioner researcher, interviewed service users and service providers to evaluate an innovative new service. The data showed that the service users were not satisfied and that their perception of the service was very different from that held by the service providers. The service providers were displeased about these findings. They felt that the research was unjust and in retrospect wished they had not taken part. They did not want the results to be made public.

 Should Jim publicise the findings?

In order to retain professional integrity Jim has no option but to report the findings as accurately as possible, but this case illustrates how difficult this can be when research participants or research sponsors do not like the research results. Few would argue that the results of research should not be in the public domain but this may not always be in the control of the practitioner researcher. The research contract may stipulate that the funding agency will decide how to disseminate the findings or a line manager may limit or even prohibit dissemination of findings. Jim's research had been commissioned by the service provider. He presented a report of his findings to them and was discouraged from more widespread dissemination and complied in recognition that to do otherwise would leave him vulnerable to negative feedback from colleagues and managers.

Retaining professional standards can also be a challenge if the practitioner researcher is funded by an organisation with a clear commercial interest in the outcome, such as a study of smoking-related disease funded by a tobacco company. The practitioner researcher may feel under some pressure to come up with the 'right results'.

The relationship with research participants and responsibilities to them as well as anonymity, privacy and confidentiality all relate to the need to ensure that the practitioner researcher's quest for the advancement of knowledge does not override the rights of others. Key to all ethical guidelines is the need to ensure that the physical and psychological well-being of research participants is not adversely affected by the research. Research participants should be treated with respect and dignity and participation should be based on freely given informed consent. Participants should never be coerced into taking part in research and need to be aware that they are free to withdraw from the research at any time.

Participants should understand that they will be given anonymity and that their privacy and confidentiality will be maintained. The practitioner researcher should also inform the participant of their rights under the Data Protection Act. Anonymity can be particularly challenging in a number of practice settings. Research practitioners often conduct small-scale research in their place of work. Even though they may go to great lengths to retain the anonymity of the research participants they may unwittingly collect data that makes the participant identifiable. It would, for example, be relatively simple to identify a teacher from an anonymous survey that collects details of the age, gender, location of school and current role of the research participants. A 45 year old female head teacher in a particular town may well be identifiable to others.

Covert research where the research is conducted without the knowledge of research participants is the subject of much debate as it by definition transgresses the 'informed consent' principle. Most professional bodies would rather avoid this type of approach although it is sometimes seen to be acceptable if the topic is sufficiently important and there is no other way of collecting the data. There are a number of topics that may fall into this category such as health care workers' hygiene practices in the workplace. In this scenario, staff will be likely to change their practice if they know that they are being observed and far more accurate data will be collected by covert research.

6.3   DOING ETHICAL RESEARCH

All professional practitioners should operate within the ethical codes of their regulatory bodies and those that they are contractually bound to by their employers. Issues such as confidentiality and treating clients with dignity and respect are well understood and uniformly practised by professionals working in health education and social care. What is often not understood, however, is the distinction between practice ethics and research ethics.

In the health field a practitioner may instigate radical change in the organisation or delivery of care which may have a profound impact on the client. Generally, the only approval that is required will be from the practitioner's line manager. However, if the practitioner is conducting research, formal approval is required for any research that collects primary data from either medical records or health care workers or patients.

Further ethical issues arise for practitioner researchers who are conducting research in their own research environment. Being a researcher is quite different from being a practitioner. The prime distinction between being a practitioner and a researcher is related to one's relationship with clients. A practitioner by definition provides a service to the client whereas a researcher rarely does. However, both practitioner researchers and their clients may have trouble disassociating the two. It is, for example, difficult for a well-established carer/service user or teacher/pupil relationship to change because the practitioner happens to be engaged in a research project. The research participants may not even realise that the practitioner's role has shifted as the activity of the practitioner and researcher are often not dissimilar. For example, a client assessment interview carried out by a practitioner may be very similar to a patient experience interview carried out by a practitioner researcher as both may involve asking the client very similar questions.

Involving a client in practitioner research will affect the relationship and this throws up a number of ethical issues. First, does a practitioner researcher approach a client to see whether they would like to collaborate with the research?

The basic principles of ethical recruitment are that the research participant:

- Is well-informed about the study in language that they can understand
- Is not coerced either directly or indirectly into taking part
- Gives their full consent voluntarily
- Understands that they are free to withdraw from the study at any time
- Is given assurance that their participation will not affect their care

Practitioner researchers need to be aware that using clients as research participants will impact upon their relationship with the client. It is therefore extremely important that the practitioner researcher consults with the service user about the implications before, during and after the research and monitors the impact throughout. These issues may be particularly pronounced in qualitative research or an action research project as these may involve the collection of data about service user experiences that would not normally form part of the dialogue with the health or social care professional (Butler, 2003).

Box 6.5   Key questions to consider when involving clients in research

- How should you ask clients if they want to be involved in research?
- How will it affect your relationship if they accept?
- How will it affect your relationship if they decline?
- What if their interest wanes during the course of the project?

Confusion of role may also occur for practitioner researchers who use colleagues as research participants. This can be particularly problematic for practitioner researchers who line-manage people they wish to include in research. Inviting someone you line-manage to take part in your research is clearly not a neutral invitation and raises ethical questions. To what extent can the invitation be refused? And to what extent will the participant provide 'truthful' information?

All research is biased but it needs to be recognised that the bias is likely to be even more pronounced if a practitioner researcher is conducting research in his or her own workplace. In some extreme cases, such as a manager using his or her staff as research participants, the bias may be so pronounced as to throw doubt upon the veracity of the results.

One way to overcome this problem is for practitioner researchers to conduct research somewhere other than their own place of work. This may of course not be feasible and may not be desirable for all practitioner researchers as their motivation for research is usually to improve the service they provide. Thus some practitioner researchers may view their research as less relevant if conducted anywhere other than their own place of work. We have also seen in Chapter 4 how familiarity with a workplace gives the practitioner researcher unique insight into the 'shadow side' of organisations.

Some practitioner researchers try to minimise the impact of prior relationships with research participants by excluding their own clients from their research and using clients of their colleagues. A nurse may find a different ward to the one they works in to conduct their research. Or a teacher researcher may conduct research with another class to the one that they teach assuming that going to a different school is not an option. However, other practitioner researchers, particularly those using an action research model, specifically select their own clients and colleagues on the grounds that changing the relationship and changing practice is the central purpose of the research.

There are then clear advantages and disadvantages for practitioner researchers conducting research in their own place of work. These need to be considered carefully in advance in the light of the overall purpose of the research and the impact of the practitioner researcher's own position upon the quality of the data collected.

6.4   OBTAINING ETHICAL APPROVAL

Whilst practitioner researchers are able to draw upon their professional experience and training to understand the concepts underlying ethical research, the process of obtaining ethical and research governance approval is often unfamiliar. The idea of having research scrutinised and judged by a committee is feared by many, particularly fledgling practitioner researchers who are aware of their vulnerability when faced with powerful committees equipped with an arsenal of professional members, experts and statutory powers. This fear is reinforced by the battle scars and stories of 'survivors' who have 'done battle' with the committees previously. Many of these stories come close to acquiring the status of urban myth and are no doubt greatly embellished as they are told and retold over the years.

Practitioner researchers need to be aware that obtaining REC approval is not a rubber-stamping exercise. Some committees can and do provide harsh criticism, which is not necessarily sensitively delivered. Many researchers find the process disempowering and disheartening.

Case Study:
A bad experience with a REC

I received a phone call from Mark, a senior manager studying for his doctorate, who had just come out of a meeting with a REC who were discussing his research. As his supervisor, I had not accompanied Mark to this meeting as I knew him to be articulate, research literate and familiar with committees. Moreover he had written a first class research protocol which had already been approved with flying colours by the R&D committee of the organisation in which he worked. When Mark called me he was clearly in an agitated state and told

(Continued)

(Continued)

me that the ethics committee had not given approval for his research. They had taken issue on a number of counts ranging from overall research design through to data collection instruments selected and questioned whether the research subjects were too vulnerable to be included in a research project. There had been more than 10 people on the committee, only one of whom had gone to any lengths to make Mark feel at all welcome. All those who commented on his application had been overtly critical and two had been actively hostile. He felt 'incandescent' with rage and demoralised. Mark described the experience as 'the most humiliating I have ever experienced in all my years working as a clinician and senior manager'.

Practitioner researchers should however be reassured that most researchers gain the approval they need for their research. Scrutiny of research projects by a number of committees is generally performed sensitively and conscientiously. In order to minimise the difficulties there are also some strategies that the practitioner researcher can draw upon (see Box 6.6).

Box 6.6   Strategies to help the approval process

- Seek advice when completing approval application forms
- Find out about the composition of the relevant committee
- Be prepared to defend the proposed research robustly
- Practise answering possible questions that may be asked
- Listen to the advice of the committee
- Be prepared to compromise

Practitioner researchers should seek advice prior to seeking approval. Many will have a research supervisor to consult and many organisations have a research manager. Details about the relevant committee will often be available on the web. It is also advisable to have a practice run-through beforehand in order to answer questions authoritatively. Robust defence of the research design may be required but it is also important to listen to the concerns and suggestions of the committee and to be prepared to make compromises.

Qualitative research and action research are often particularly vulnerable to harsh handling from approval committees, who tend to adhere to objective world models traditionally associated with medical RECs. In recognition of the limited understanding of qualitative research that can be encountered, Walker et al. (2005) offer guidelines for the ethical review of qualitative research, which practitioner researchers would be well advised to consult. At another level, the practitioner researcher must be prepared for the culture of the committee. Approaching it as an interview may set the right tone. The case study below is a quote from a practitioner researcher reflecting on his encounter with an REC.

Case Study:
Handling committees – the interview

[T]he committee is very traditional and male orientated (with only one fairly unfeminine female member) who believe scientific rigour constitutes a strong ethical backbone to a project. They are, however, unfamiliar with qualitative research methods, which is actually an opportunity for a candidate, since in traditional medical fashion they [the Committee] can be taken in by bullshit if stated confidently. To clarify issues that the Committee might view as potential 'problems' with the method prior to the meeting I brought along the biggest book on qualitative research methods I could muster as a 'totem' of authenticity and duly quoted sections pertaining to the relevant issue. They said thank you for being so precise and succinct!

The practitioner researcher must approach the interview with confidence in him-or herself as a researcher and because of the quality of their research proposal. The practitioner researcher in the case study was aware that 'He operated quite comfortably in this environment' to the extent that he even noted he was wearing similar attire to the Chair of the committee. He also went on to say that 'Before I went in, a nurse was waiting her turn after me and expressed concern that she would feel intimidated by the maleness of the committee. I naïvely suggested that it was unlikely to be the case but afterwards upon reflection I can quite see that she may have had legitimate worries.'

6.5   STRIKING A BALANCE BETWEEN BUREAUCRACY AND ETHICAL RESEARCH

Has Research Governance Gone Too Far?

The Research Governance Framework and RECs described earlier were introduced to improve the ethical and scientific quality of research conducted in the NHS and to safeguard the well-being of research participants. These are clearly of primary importance in research. However, a Department of Health review makes reference to frequent complaints from researchers about the 'increased bureaucracy' involved in research (DoH, 2005a: 8).

From the case study describing excessive bureaucracy at the beginning of this chapter, such comments are well justified.

The amount of resources required for practitioner researchers to make the relevant ethics and research governance applications calls into question the ethics of spending large amounts of public money on such activities. If added to this is a proportion of the salaries of the many R&D employees in organisations who are involved in the approval process, the cost of obtaining approval is astronomical and cannot be justified. The Department of Health (2005a) have recently made a number of recommendations relating to the bureaucracy of the local and national structures that the practitioner researcher has to engage with. The process should be far less onerous when the recommendations are implemented. These include:

- A triage system whereby not all research projects would be sent to RECs
- A streamlined form
- Adoption of common national systems by NHS research hosts
- A reduced number of RECs with broader and paid membership
- Training for REC members to reduce inconsistency
- The introduction of 'Scientific Officers' to support the work of the RECs

An implementation plan is under way (see www.corec.org.uk/consultation/ ImplementationPlanConsultation.pdf). It is likely that in the next few years there will be a reduction in the bureaucracy involved in obtaining approval to undertake research.

Avoiding bureaucracy

Practitioner researchers can and do complain that research bureaucracy spoils research creativity. Certainly it can act as an unwelcome check for the practitioner researcher. It has also led to a number of strategies designed to avoid much of the bureaucratic process.

The first strategy is to draw a clear distinction between research and practitioner research, as discussed in Chapter 5. Practitioner research would normally entail reflection on practice concepts or phenomena in the context of a systematic review of the literature, using practice experience to provide examples of a particular phenomenon. Such a study would not normally be classified by COREC as research and would therefore not be subjected to the rigorous bureaucratic procedures described above.

A second strategy is to label some research-type activities as 'audit' rather than 'research' as there is a grey area between the two (Wade, 2005). Audits are deemed to lie outside the COREC framework and are seen as part of good or even statutory practice rather than research. Some practitioner researchers take advantage of the fact that audit and research may involve very similar types of activity. Take, for example, a client satisfaction survey. This may be defined as audit or research depending on the organisation in which it is conducted, the purpose for which it is being carried out and the type of questions that are being asked. Yet the categorisation will determine whether it is within the research governance framework and its cumbersome bureaucracy or the audit structures in the organisation.

Practitioner researchers may be genuinely unsure whether they are doing audit or research and they would be advised to consult sources defining audit and research and the differences between them that we raised in Chapter 4 see www.nwlh.nhs.uk [for further clarification]. However, Wade (2005) suggests that the distinction between audit and research is often blurred and that therefore ethical or moral considerations should determine the level of scrutiny a project requires rather than an arbitrary categorisation. Whatever the categorisation, ethical standards apply equally for audit and research.

It is not ethical for a practitioner researcher to categorise any research activity as audit or practitioner research simply to avoid a lengthy bureaucratic process and we are not recommending this strategy. However, neither is it ethical to stop undertaking research because the bureaucracy is so overwhelming that the practitioner researcher feels frightened and powerless. We would encourage practitioner researchers to seek advice from an R&D manager in their organisation, their colleagues and their line manager to ensure that their research is ethical and has the requisite approvals.

Don't Throw the Baby Out with the Bathwater

This chapter has adopted a sceptical stance about the onerous approval process currently in place for health and social care research carried out in the statutory sector, even suggesting that national structures are squeezing the life blood out of research. The national research structures also act as an obstacle to joint working. Practitioners are constantly being urged to work together more closely yet the lack of coordination related to research regulations in different agencies makes this very difficult. We would hope that in the future there will be more joined-up working between the different bureaucracies in order to reduce the number of hoops that the practitioner researcher has to jump through.

Despite our scepticism about the existing structures, we would not wish to downplay the centrality of ethical considerations when conducting research. It is of primary importance that the practitioner researcher recognises the distinction between research ethics and practice ethics. The current checks are in place due to the failure of professionals adequately to police their own research in the past. We therefore recognise the need for ethical approval for research and the need for governance to protect the researcher and the research participants. We would, however, welcome a lighter touch from the national structures and we look forward to seeing the fruits of on-going developments to make the structures more coherent and less onerous to the researcher.

SUMMARY

- All research should be 'ethical' and practitioner researchers should look to their professional regulatory body for guidance
- Examples of poor research practice in the past show that there is a need for a mandatory system to ensure that all research meets appropriate ethical, practical and professional standards
- There is a danger that systems to safeguard the research participant can become too bureaucratic
- The process of obtaining approval for research can be lengthy and disheartening, but it is a necessary part of the process and may serve to sharpen the details of research

FURTHER READING

Fraser, D.M. (1997) 'Ethical dilemmas and practical problems for the practitioner researcher', *Educational Action Research,* **5 (1): 161–71**

This paper looks at the dilemmas and problems the author encountered when undertaking an evaluation of an innovative midwifery education programme in her own school.

Wade, D.T. (2005) 'Ethics, audit and research: all shades of grey', *British Medical Journal,* **330: 468–71**

A thoughtful discussion of the boundaries (or lack of them) between audit and research.

7
Undertaking Research

This chapter focuses on the practical issues encountered during the research journey. It stresses the need for careful planning at all stages, from the design of a good 'road map' before setting out, a clear route master and careful sign-posting while on the way, to contingency plans for when the journey does not go according to plan. It covers:

> ⇨ Research design
> ⇨ Developing a research proposal
> ⇨ Fixed protocols and flexible research
> ⇨ Time management and Gantt charts

7.1 RESEARCH DESIGN

The Research Proposal

A research proposal is a brief description of the proposed research that is clear enough and provides enough detail to answer the following questions.

- Why is the proposed research important?
- How does the research relate (and add) to the previous literature?
- What are the research aims?
- Can all the research questions be answered by the research design?
- Is the proposed plan of research feasible?
- Can the research be done with the time and resources proposed?
- Is the research ethical and within the research governance framework?
- Are the researchers sufficiently well placed and competent to conduct the research?

The questions seem relatively straightforward but many research proposals fail to provide adequate answers. A proposal that clearly addresses all the above questions will result in much more straightforward research. There is no set format for a research proposal and different organisations often request somewhat different information. All research proposals will contain the elements listed in Box 7.1, although the amount of detail required will vary considerably.

Box 7.1   Elements of the research proposal

- Title
- Background
- Aims and objectives
- Plan or method
- Timetable
- Dissemination
- Ethical issues
- Budget
- References

The Research Framework

In order to write the research proposal a clear research framework is required. Many research textbooks provide a framework for undertaking research and we have drawn upon a number of these, in particular Robson (2002) and Creswell (2003), to develop our own framework. At its simplest this framework suggests a series of questions that should be asked to clarify the design of the research.

What is the purpose of the research?   We have stressed throughout this book that there has to be a purpose to undertaking research. At its simplest, the purpose of research may be defined as generating new knowledge. However, the generation of new knowledge may be undertaken for a variety of reasons. These may include introduction of new procedures or empowering particular groups of people. The practitioner researcher must be able to clarify the purpose of the research and to recognise that it has a goal (see Chapter 1).

In terms of building the research purpose into the research proposal outlined in Box 7.1, one would expect the purpose to feature in the 'Title' and

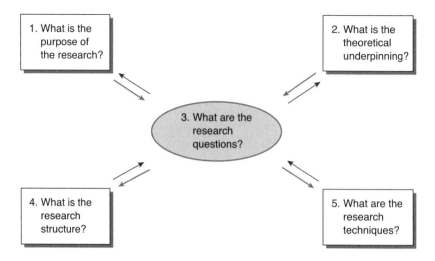

FIGURE 7.1   *The research framework*

also in 'Aims'. The 'Title' should describe the main focus of the study and what will be unique about it and should be closely related to the research 'Aim'.

What is the theoretical underpinning?   Any problem can be seen from a number of theoretical perspectives. As we explored in Chapter 1, the practitioner researcher can frame problems at a meta-level from a positivist, social constructional or constructivist view of reality. This becomes a way of viewing the problem but also a theoretical framework for the type of research to be undertaken.

In this way practitioner researchers not only have a theoretical framework for understanding an issue but also have a theoretical framework for undertaking the research.

The theoretical framework is also affected by the purpose of the research. So to answer the question 'Why are boys from Afro-Caribbean backgrounds more likely to be excluded from schools than their peers?' different theoretical frameworks will suggest different purposes for the research. The goal of the psychologist may be to investigate the self-esteem of black pupils. The goal of the social worker may be to investigate stress levels in teachers, whilst the goal of the teachers might be to investigate the culture of the schools. Each of these different goals leads to different types of research. The social workers might wish to undertake some emancipatory research with teachers, whilst the psychologist might wish to measure self-esteem (and introduce a programme to change it). Meanwhile the teachers might be involved in some action research on the school as a system.

In constructing the research proposal the 'Background' describes the rationale for the research, the theoretical underpinning and how it relates to the existing literature. Key texts will be noted here. It needs to show clearly how the proposed research emerges from a review of the literature and cites the research within relevant academic and applied literature.

What are the Research Questions? The theoretical framework and the purpose of the research will underpin the formation of the research questions and the research questions are in turn closely linked to the research methodology.

In the terminology of the research proposal (see Box 7.1), the research questions are derived from the 'Aims and Objectives'. The research 'Aim' should state clearly what the study is intended to find out. The research objectives are specific issues to be looked at by the work, which are related to the overall aim. Objectives are generally related to specific empirical outcomes and form the basis for the 'research questions'.

Qualitative and quantitative research have different ways of writing research questions (see Creswell, 2003 for a full explanation). In qualitative research, Creswell suggests that the central question or 'Aim' is as open as possible and relates to the methodology to be used as described in the case study below.

Case Study:
A phenomenological study

Central question: What are the experiences of physically disabled children moving from a special to a mainstream school?

The sub-questions or 'objectives' then focus on particular areas that the research will explore. For example, the sub-questions might be:

- What is the impact on relationships – both old and new?
- How do the pupils feel physically – in particular, tiredness?
- How does it change the way pupils see themselves?
- How do families react?
- How do pupils feel about their independence?

In this qualitative research, none of the above research questions have yes/no or right/wrong answers. In contrast, in quantitative research the convention is to have specific research hypotheses, which the research will either prove or disprove. Hypotheses are usually based on previous research and theory and are predictions the researcher has about the connection between two or more variables. A hypothesis, is usually written as a null hypothesis, which makes the prediction that there is no relationship between the variables.

Case Study:
A quantitative study

The null hypothesis: There is no difference between the academic achievement of children with physical disabilities in special and mainstream schools.
   The sub-hypotheses will then break this down into readily testable hypotheses. For example:

   Controlling for differences in attainment at baseline tests taken when the child begins school aged 5:

   • There is no difference in the SATs scores of children with physical disabilities in special and mainstream schools at ages 7 and 11
   • There is no difference in IQ scores between children with physical disabilities in special and mainstream schools
   • There is no difference in GCSE grades attained at 16 years between children with physical disabilities in special and mainstream schools

---

What is the Research Structure?   The research structure and the research techniques described below form the basis of what is often termed the 'Plan' or 'Method' in a research proposal. This area is key in terms of assessing the feasibility of the research and many proposals fail to provide sufficient detail. A detailed plan of research is the most challenging aspect of writing a research proposal for the practitioner researcher. Practitioner researchers need to understand research design before starting to research. Robson (2002) distinguishes between fixed and flexible design.

Fixed design
• Tight pre-specification before data collection
• Data usually in the form of numbers (quantitative)

Flexible design
• Design evolves during data collection and analysis
• Data usually in the form of words (qualitative)

   A fixed structure is when the practitioner researcher has a very clear plan for undertaking the research before it is started. This is contrasted with more flexible research that is undertaken by building up the structure incrementally and flexibly. A good example of this is action research, where each stage of the research depends upon the previous stage.

Once the design of the research is developed, the final stage of the framework laid out in Figure 7.1 can be addressed – what are the techniques for gathering the data?

What are the research techniques?   There are many different research techniques. Among those most commonly used are:

- Observation
- Interviewing
- Surveys and questionnaires
- Focus groups
- Attitude scales
- Standardised tests

There are many others and each of the categories listed above has a number of subcategories. Numerous research methods textbooks describe these techniques and research training courses are readily available.

Beyond the research framework   In addition to the research framework, a research proposal should also contain the following: a budget, a discussion of ethical issues related to the research, a plan for analysis and dissemination of the research results and key references.

The budget details required may be quite minimal for a student doing a research dissertation, for example, cost of mailing 200 questionnaires @ 25 pence each = £50. For a major project funded by a research council, however, the cost may total hundreds of thousands of pounds and a detailed budget stretching over several pages is required to enable the funding agency to account for spending public money.

Forward planning is again key for this aspect as researchers have to estimate in great detail the cost of the research. This requires thinking in advance about staffing requirements, the number of phone calls that are likely to be made during the course of the research, how much travelling will be required, how much the equipment will cost etc. The following expenditures would normally be included:

- Details of posts and salaries, including on-costs and increments
- Travel costs
- Consumables (stationery, photocopying, postage, phone)
- Equipment purchase and maintenance cost
- Overheads charged by the host institution to cover accommodation, heating etc.
- Dissemination costs, such as hosting an end-of-project workshop

The budget for research is integral to the size and scope of the research. Generally research funded by a national or international body is larger in scope and more expensive. In general, the greatest expense by far is researchers' salaries. In addition, research establishments generally charge overheads for research.

It is necessary to think through all potential costs. Research funding agencies will generally not provide additional funding if the money runs out before the research is completed so it is therefore important to ask for sufficient funding. Asking for too much may discourage the funding agency from funding it at all and it is also common practice for research councils to ask for a return of unused funds at the end of the project.

A research proposal includes a discussion of ethical issues relating to the research as well as the procedure for obtaining ethical approval to proceed. (See Chapter 6 for further details relating to this aspect.)

A research proposal also includes details about how the results will be analysed and how the research will be disseminated. It will state how the different stakeholders are to be informed about the results of the research and note the appropriate format for this. (See Chapter 10 for further discussion of this aspect.)

Finally, all research proposals should include references that are of key importance to the research. References should always be in a standard citation format and be relevant to the proposal.

7.2   DEVELOPING A RESEARCH PROPOSAL – AN EXAMPLE

There are a number of common pitfalls to avoid when writing a research proposal. There is a tendency for research proposals to:

- Have vague and ill-defined aims
- Lack detail about the research design
- Be overly ambitious and unrealistic in terms of scope and timetable

Defining Aims and Objectives

Case Study:
Betsy's aims and objectives

Betsy is a social worker who works as part of a multidisciplinary team to support HIV-positive adolescents. She is particularly interested in conducting research that will identify strategies to maximise the young people's awareness and

(Continued)

(Continued)

practice of safer sexual behaviour. She has read the relevant literature and is ready to write her research proposal. She starts off with the aims and objectives of the research.

Aim: To develop guidelines to support safer sexual behaviour in HIV-positive adolescents

Objectives:
- To explore how HIV-positive adolescents feel about their sexuality
- To examine their knowledge of sexual transmission of HIV
- To assess their sexual behaviour and the degree to which it is 'safe'
- To see whether sexual behaviour is linked to their self-esteem
- To identify what help they would like to assist them in achieving safer sexual behaviour whilst retaining their self-esteem

 How clear and feasible are these aims and objectives?

The aim of Betsy's research seems relatively straightforward although it is vague and gives few clues about what type of support/intervention the research is working towards.

The objectives she has identified, which will form the basis of the research questions, reveal a lack of focus. She is interested in achieving safer sexual behaviour and therefore lists the adolescents' attitudes, knowledge and behaviour as key objectives in her research. She is also concerned about their self-esteem as they develop their sexual identities. And finally, she wants to know what they feel they would like from service providers to assist them to develop their sexuality. In trying to address all these issues, Betsy's research lacks focus and is likely to find adequate answers to none of the questions the research raises. She would do well to address one issue only and research this in some detail.

Planning

Common problems when planning research and determining the research structure and techniques include:

- Failure to explain key details, such as how respondents are to be recruited, what questions will be asked, or how questionnaires will be designed
- Underestimation of the time and effort involved in particular aspects of the research, such as recruiting participants or writing up the results

- Failure to recognise barriers and delays that are outside the control of the researcher, such as the time it can take to obtain the necessary approval to undertake the research
- Failure to charge for routine research expenses, such as funding to attend conferences or to buy vital equipment
- Inadequate consideration of ethical problems associated with the research

Returning to Betsy, let us assume that she decides to focus upon sexual behaviour and decides that a qualitative study using focus groups is the most appropriate.

Case Study:
Betsy's research plan

- A qualitative study using focus groups
- Recruit five focus groups of 8–10 adolescents
- Recruit clients from the service I work for
- Ask them questions about their sexual behaviour
- Tape-record and transcribe the focus groups

 ☐ What are your thoughts about Betsy's research design?

Betsy's first rudimentary ideas about the research plan are very loose. Key to the success of any research project is a full and detailed plan of how the research will be carried out. Research proposals that lack a detailed plan are unlikely to achieve their goal and hardly ever receive funding.

Betsy therefore needs to think things through further. She needs a rationale for her decision to use focus groups. Focus groups may be perceived to be a threatening forum for HIV-positive young people to talk candidly about sexual behaviour. They may also encourage 'boastful' behaviour and exaggerations. They may work, but due to the highly sensitive subject a lot of background thought and planning will first be required.

Betsy needs to consider whether the number of participants she hopes to recruit (40–50) is realistic. What proportion will this represent of the adolescent clients of the service? What proportion of these will agree to take part in the research and in addition will their parents also consent? What proportion of these will agree to take part in a focus group with their peers?

Careful thought is also required about how to recruit participants and how they should be constituted. Who should approach them about the research?

Would colleagues be prepared to assist with recruitment? Should young men and women be recruited to the same focus group? Should young adolescents be recruited to the same group as older adolescents?

She will also need to determine how the focus groups should be organised and how material can be developed to stimulate discussion of the topic in a general non-threatening way. She will need to think about the impact of peer pressure and how to ensure that participants express the full range of views not just those that are deemed to be acceptable to their peers. Finally, she will need to think about how the data will be analysed.

As part of the detailed plan, a timetable of work is required. This is discussed in greater depth in section 7.4.

7.3   FIXED PROTOCOLS AND FLEXIBLE RESEARCH

Flexibility: a Key Requisite

Detailed planning is key to the smooth running of research. However, research takes place in an unpredictable and uncertain world and even the most meticulously planned projects will encounter unforeseen barriers. Experienced researchers know that as a result of the unexpected, research generally takes longer than originally projected and often costs more too.

It is not feasible to plan for every eventuality and therefore practitioner researchers do have to be prepared to be flexible. In some research designs, such as action research, flexibility may be an important component in the process as each stage depends upon the outcome of the preceding stage. But even in projects using a fixed design the research rarely follows the research proposal to the letter once implementation begins. We focus here on the most common sources of the unexpected and the unplanned faced by the practitioner researcher.

Box 7.2   Common obstacles for practitioner researchers

- The changing landscape of the research setting
  - External forces
  - Change of role at work
- Time
  - Underestimated through inexperience
  - The disappearing research participant
  - Research governance and ethics
- Research/life balance
  - Unforeseen life events

The Changing Landscape of the Research Setting

Natural disasters and war notwithstanding, research activity in a service setting is particularly vulnerable to political changes that lead to changes in policy and a reconfiguration of services. For example, education research on the effectiveness of separate middle schools for children aged 9–13 is going to be ruined if a new Minister of Education decides to abolish middle schools. Likewise research evaluating the effectiveness of a residential support service for looked after children with complex needs will be left high and dry if the local authority decides that they can no longer resource such a service. Whilst these examples are extreme, health and social services in the UK are largely characterised by being in a constant state of change and reorganisation. Thus all practitioner researchers have to try to assess, before starting any research, the degree to which the service they are researching is likely to continue in its current form and for how long it is likely to do so.

Just as services may change so may the practitioners who staff them. Whereas a practitioner researcher may have felt well supported in their work environment to carry out research, a new line manager may actively discourage and disallow time for research.

Practitioner researchers may move or be moved to a new role. They may get promotion, they may be asked to take on a new role or new job opportunities may arise elsewhere. Whether volitional or not, a change in role will inevitably impact on the research. 'I've got a new job now and want to research something different' is not an uncommon refrain from the practitioner researcher.

Time

'I never realised it would take so long!' People often fail to understand why research is such a costly exercise and as a result much research funded by lay organisations is often under-resourced. The reason for the relatively high cost of research is that it is a time-consuming activity and time costs money, in particular the salaries of those employed on the project. Few people comprehend how much time research can take without experiencing it first-hand.

Robson (2002: 447) has noted that 'Trying to do a systematic enquiry on top of normal commitments is very difficult.' Practitioner researchers undertaking research often underestimate the amount of time that will be required to complete their research. They underestimate the time it takes:

• To set up the research and gain the cooperation of all the stakeholders involved in the research
• To obtain ethics and formal organisational approval

- To recruit people to participate and collect data from them
- To code data and enter it onto the appropriate software
- To write research reports

We have discussed the lengthy time it can take obtaining the requisite approvals in Chapter 6. Once approval is obtained cooperation of the stakeholders is then required and this can also take time. Normally the practitioner researcher is well placed to establish the requisite cooperative relationships for research, but an overstretched line manager, a jealous colleague or a concerned service user can cause delay.

Then there is the recruitment of participants, and the 'disappearing research participant' is a common setback. Researchers frequently fail to estimate accurately the number of participants who: fit the inclusion/exclusion criteria; agree to take part in the research; are accessible at a mutually convenient time; present for interview at the appointed time; return their questionnaire etc. The research is unlikely to be high priority for research participants and few are willing to make special journeys, keep diary appointments and spend lengthy amounts of time assisting the researcher with data collection.

Processing the data and writing the research reports are further sources of frequent delay. Each activity requires painstaking and careful thought and cannot be achieved overnight. Neither is well suited to the occasional hour or two fitted into the already busy schedule of the practitioner researcher. They require dedicated, concentrated research time and the practitioner researcher would be well advised to build this into the schedule at the outset.

 Thinking back to Betsy and the research she is planning:

- ☐ Who will she need to talk to in order to get cooperation to carry out her research?
- ☐ How long will it take her to get ethics approval to carry out research in this sensitive area with a very vulnerable group of young people?
- ☐ How many adolescents and their parents will she need to talk to in order to recruit a sufficient sample for just one focus group?
- ☐ How long will it take her to transcribe the data and master an appropriate software package?
- ☐ How many days should she allocate for processing and analysing the data and writing up the results?

There are no precise answers to questions such as these, but the practitioner researcher would do well to spend time making estimates that are as accurate as they can be.

In this case, Betsy will need to list the stakeholders that she needs to get 'on-side' with her research. This will include her colleagues, the clients, the clients' parents, her line manager and her employing organisation. She will need to work out who to speak to and how long this will take.

Ethics forms get ever longer and are ever more time-consuming to complete. They need to be submitted usually two weeks before the committee meets. It is not uncommon for changes to be requested following the meeting. It is rare for the process of obtaining approvals to take less than three months.

Recruiting participants and collecting data can be extremely time-consuming. Betsy's study is not large but she may have to speak to a large number of potential participants before a sufficient number agree to take part. This stage is likely to take at least another three months.

Betsy then needs to transcribe the data and find out how to use a software analysis package. How long this takes will depend on whether she has funds to pay someone to assist with transcription. In general transcribing a tape takes at least four times longer than the interview itself.

The process of analysis and the writing up of the results usually take about as much time as all the other stages put together. Betsy hopes to complete this research in a year. It seems that she will be hard pressed to do so.

Research/Life Balance

All researchers have to find a healthy work/life balance and this is a challenge due to the unpredictable nature of much research and the tight deadlines that are built into projects. It is even more of a challenge if unforeseen life events (both positive and negative) occur during the research. Due to the relatively lengthy nature of a research project an unplanned life event is practically a certainty.

Any number of real-life incidents can impede research and prevent it from running to plan. Similar problems are a common feature of almost all research, but they have a different impact on practitioner researchers as research is unlikely to be their only activity. Also, by definition, practitioner researchers have a day job to perform. Full-time researchers have little option but to resolve the research problems they face during the course of their research. Practitioner researchers, however, have far less impetus to do so as the research is unlikely to be their highest priority. Practitioner researchers are thus particularly vulnerable to unplanned events such as those in Figure 7.2 as they have to juggle life, work and research. They have to keep all three balls in the air and, should they have to drop one, it is most likely to be the research.

Despite the many pitfalls that can beset research, the problems are generally surmountable. With careful planning and judicious time management, practitioner researchers can overcome obstacles and complete their research.

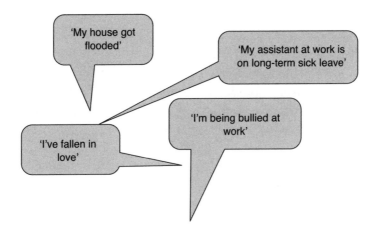

FIGURE 7.2   *Unplanned events*

7.4   TIME MANAGEMENT AND GANTT CHARTS

The Need for Tight Time Management

Research, as we have seen, is complex in that it involves a number of different stages. Any research project therefore takes a great deal of thought and time and cannot be completed overnight. Typically research projects take a minimum of six months and often continue for up to five years. Longitudinal research looking at changes over time may continue for much longer than this.

Ideally the length of the project will depend on what is required to complete the research. The reality for the practitioner researcher, however, is to start with the question 'How much time do I have?' and then plan the research to make sure it fits into the time available.

A practitioner researcher doing a research project as part of a degree may have to complete the research in nine months and may have only one day a week to spend on it. The planning therefore needs to ensure that the research can be completed in 30–35 days and the size and scope of the research adjusted accordingly.

Strategies have been developed to assist the researcher with time management and it is vital the practitioner researcher uses such strategies from the outset. Careful time management will ensure that the research proposal is feasible within the available resources. It does not take a lot of research experience to know that ten days is not sufficient to recruit 50 participants and conduct in-depth interviews with them. Yet a lot of practitioner researchers unwittingly make such claims and this could be avoided with judicious use of a time management chart.

Constructing a Gantt Chart

Gantt charts are a very convenient means of planning a project. The chart was devised by Henry Gantt (1861–1919), an American engineer who used these charts for planning building ships during the First World War.

Gantt charts display project tasks and milestones along a horizontal timescale. Such charts give visual clarity and can include information density. They provide an excellent overview of a research project and enable the practitioner researcher to sequence research activities in the right order.

Gantt charts are very useful to track and chart research timelines. They are not difficult to construct and you can create a Gantt chart in Excel or using other software and can be easily found on the web.

Case Study:
Constructing a Gantt chart for Betsy's research

	J	F	M	A	M	J	J	A	S	O	N	D
Obtain approval	8	8	8									
Recruit participants				4	8	8						
Run focus groups							4					
Process the data							4	4				
Analyse the data								4	4			
Write research report									4	8	8	
Present the findings										2	2	2

In this example the research is relatively small scale in that it is to be completed in a year. Let us assume that this is Betsy's project described above and she has two days a week to spend on the project.

(Continued)

(Continued)

- Betsy knows that this is a project in a sensitive area so she has allowed herself 3 months to obtain approval. During this time she plans to talk to colleagues and other stakeholders about her research and seek their cooperation, all of which is vital preparation for recruitment
- Once the project is approved, recruitment of participants can begin. Betsy estimates that she will need to talk to about 48 adolescents and their parents in order to recruit four focus groups (two male and two female – she hopes to have six in each). She estimates that she will talk to two potential participants each day and successfully recruit one in two. She therefore allows three months for recruitment. She allows for fewer days in April as she has leave booked
- The following month (July) she plans to run the focus groups and begin the transcription of the tapes
- In August she aims to complete the transcription and begin the analysis
- In September she estimates she will complete her analysis and start writing the results. This gives her over three months to finish writing up and disseminating the results

---

Case Study:
How Accurate was Betsy's Gantt chart?

	J	F	M	A	M	J	J	A	S	O	N	D	J	F
Research approval obtained	8	8	8	2										
Recruit participants				2	8	8	4							
Run focus groups							2							
Process the data							2	0	0	2				
Analyse the data								0	0	0				
Write research report									0	0	14	8	4	0
Present the findings										0	0	0	4	4

(Continued)

(Continued)

- In reality obtaining approval to start the project took rather longer than anticipated and recruitment did not begin until the end of April
- Recruitment was slow and Betsy only recruited one in four of those she talked to. She decided to reduce the number of focus groups from four to two in order to keep to the timetable
- Each focus group took two hours, creating 20 hours of transcription work (she is a slow typist)
- She went on holiday in August (which she had forgotten to plan for in her original time chart) and returned early as her father had been taken ill. She did not return to work until the family crisis was stabilised by mid-September. She had such a backlog of work that she was not able to return to her research until October
- She fell further behind schedule when writing the report. She took two weeks' leave but was still not able to complete the writing in time or complete her plans for dissemination
- She finally completed two months behind schedule. She forgot to take account of her summer holiday but could not have foreseen the disruption caused by family events. She also underestimated the time it would take to write up the results

A Gantt chart does not ensure that the project will be completed on time. It does, however, enable careful planning prior to the start of the project and also adjustments to be made as the project progresses. A Gantt chart helps enormously with the task of making realistic assessments of the time each stage of the research will take. It will also assist the practitioner researcher to manage obstacles that present themselves along the way.

SUMMARY

- Writing a research proposal requires thinking about the beginning, course and end product of the research. Each research project needs clarity from the outset about where it is going and a detailed blueprint about how it is going to get there
- It is important to use a framework to determine the research design. This will guide the definition of the purpose and theoretical underpinning of the research. It will inform the development of research questions which will assist the development of the structure and techniques of the research

- Research in the real world rarely goes according to plan and unforeseen obstacles may cause delay. These obstacles may be personal, work- or research-related. It is important for research to be meticulously planned in order to respond effectively when it does not go according to plan
- A detailed timetable such as a Gantt chart is a prerequisite for a well-planned research project

FURTHER READING

Locke, L.F., Spirduso, W.W., and Silverman, S.J. (2000) *Proposals that Work: a Guide for Planning Dissertations and Grant Proposals.* 4th edition. Thousand Oaks, CA: Sage.

Punch, K.F. (2000) *Developing Effective Research Proposals.* London: Sage

Both books provide general guidelines and strategies for designing and preparing a research proposal and presenting it effectively. They include examples and critiques of completed proposals.

8
Service User Involvement

Service user involvement has been a cornerstone of health and social care reform over the past decade in an attempt to ensure that the organisation of services reflects consumer choice. The Department of Health talks of achieving 'a fundamental change in our relationships with patients and the public … to move from a service that does things to and for its patients to one which is patient led, where the service works with patients to support them with their health needs' (Department of Health, 2005b: 5). Parallel changes have occurred in education. Not only are parents seen as key stakeholders but also children's views are increasingly seen as important. The United Nations Convention on the Rights of the Child makes reference to 'the child who is capable of forming his or her own views' and their 'right to express these views freely in all matters affecting the child' (UNICEF, 1990: article 12).

As part of involvement in care services, the service user is increasingly invited to take part in research related to services. This chapter will explore the involvement of service users in practitioner research. In particular it will focus on:

⇨ The role of the service user in research
⇨ Styles of involvement
⇨ Case studies
⇨ Establishing effective engagement
⇨ Ownership of research conducted in collaboration with service users

8.1   THE ROLE OF THE SERVICE USER IN RESEARCH

Who Are Service Users?

First we need to define who service users are and what constitutes involvement. We would class all those listed in Box 8.1 as potential service users for research.

Box 8.1   Who are service users?

- People who use health, education and social services
- Informal (unpaid) carers and parents
- Organisations that represent service users' interests

It is worth noting that, with the exception of the most socially excluded, we are all service users. The great majority of us send our children to state-funded schools, are registered as patients with a general practitioner and use health and social services as need arises. It thus follows that service users are very diverse and the stereotype of the vulnerable service user may be misleading. The service user may be highly articulate and powerful, particularly if part of collective action. For example, the parents of the children who died at Bristol Royal Infirmary grouped together to demand an inquiry about the high rates of mortality following heart operations on their children (Bristol Royal Infirmary Inquiry, 2001). This heralded the beginning of much more sophisticated audit systems to ensure far earlier identification of poor practice and the embedding of public involvement in the structures of the NHS.

Public involvement and empowerment is apparent in most public services. For example, the government's recent education reform in England is explicitly built upon the idea of parental choice about schooling for their children.

Few would deny that those in receipt of services, those who care for them and the organisations that represent their interests, should have an input into determining what services they require and how these services are delivered. Yet their role in research is more contentious. The evidence suggests that service user involvement improves the relevance and accountability of service research. It is reported to be beneficial in randomised controlled trials to assess the effectiveness of treatment (Hanley el al., 2001). Service user involvement ensures that the outcomes upon which effectiveness is assessed are relevant and meaningful to them in terms of quality of life (Chalmers, 1995). However, there is scepticism, particularly among some academic circles, about whether the service user should be involved in research at all. Although a minority of service users may be highly trained researchers, the majority are unlikely to have training in research.

In this respect there are parallels between service user researchers and practitioner researchers. In all likelihood neither are trained researchers and research is unlikely to be their main activity. And because they generally research their own area of practice and very often their own institution, practitioner researchers like service users are not likely to position themselves as objective.

However, practitioner and service user researchers share the advantage of being in a strong position to engage in research that can lead to a change in practice. Practitioner research that is conducted with service user involvement as a key stakeholder can be a powerful vehicle to promote change in practice.

The Rise of the Service User in Research

In the health field, the promotion of patient and public involvement has seen the development of national structures and services such as the Patients Advisory and Liaison Service and the Expert Patient Programme. Whilst there is scepticism about the degree of change associated with a number of service user involvement initiatives (see Bury, forthcoming), it cannot be denied that the service user is now in theory much more clearly centre stage. There are few activities related to the organisation and delivery of health and social care that do not at least pay lip service to the involvement of service users.

The aim of service user involvement in research is for service users to have a louder voice in the research that focuses on them. To achieve this requires a change in the social relations of research production in order to give control to representatives of the group who are the focus of the research. In this model the service user is less an active participant in a discrete part of the research process than a key stakeholder, an integral part of the research planning committee, who decides what needs to be researched, how it should be carried out and how the results are disseminated.

According to Beresford (2003) service user involvement is coming to be seen as a 'must-do activity' and he is concerned that this may encourage a 'tokenistic approach'. If the aim of practitioner research is to promote change to improve the quality of services, it is imperative not only to avoid token involvement but also to ensure that service users are fully on board. The following section examines styles of involvement and seeks to identify ways in which the practitioner researcher can involve the service user in a truly collaborative endeavour.

8.2 STYLES OF INVOLVEMENT

Consultation vs. Collaboration

INVOLVE, a national advisory group funded by the Department of Health, notes that involvement may take the form of consultation, collaboration or user control (www.invo.org.uk).

Box 8.2 Styles of involvement		
	Research-lead	**Role of service user**
Consultation	Researcher	Passive
Collaboration	Partnership	Active
User-controlled	Service user	Directive

Consultation tends to refer to researcher-led activities where service user involvement is fairly passive. In contrast, user-controlled research is research that is proactively led by the service user. Collaboration is pitched firmly between the two in that the research is conducted in partnership between the researcher and the service user.

The defining features of consultation are:

- Service users views are sought
- Consultation is top-down and initiated by the practitioner researcher
- The practitioner researcher makes decisions
- The distribution of power between the practitioner researcher and service user does not change

In this model, service user involvement may be seen as relatively unproblematic as it does not change the traditional research process. Service users are consulted to inform the research process and ensure that their views are represented but they are left outside the decision-making process. The consultation model of involvement is most prone to 'tokenistic' involvement.

Consultation is the easiest to achieve and has therefore been most apparent in service user involvement to date. The infrastructure to support service user involvement, at least in the health field, encourages a consultative approach and has been developed almost exclusively from the top down. Reports such as 'Creating a user-led NHS' (Department of Health, 2005b) have cascaded down and guided the development of structures to support service user involvement in the services in general and in research in particular.

The alternative approach, user-controlled research, has its origins in service user organisations and service user researchers (see Beresford, 2001). It originated in the disabled people's movement and from the outset located research within the structures of oppression and discrimination in society (see section 3.6 on 'emancipatory research'). Key elements in these emancipatory and user-controlled approaches are:

- The research is controlled by service users rather than non-service users (Turner and Beresford, 2004)
- The process of research production aims to equalise relationships between researchers and service users and between researchers and research participants
- Research is primarily concerned with making change rather than generating knowledge

This makes it quite distinct from service user consultation. A problem with the user-controlled approach for the practitioner researcher is that by definition it cannot originate with practitioner researchers unless they are concurrently service users too. However, the alternative perspective it offers and the scepticism with which it views 'traditional' service user involvement is vital to the development of a truly collaborative approach that goes beyond tokenism.

Achieving collaboration in an equal partnership with service users is a major challenge for the practitioner researcher and one that we examine in more detail below. Collaboration generally entails face-to-face interaction and shared decision-making so that the voice of the service user is heard equally with that of the researcher. However, in collaborative research it is common for the practitioner researcher rather than the service user to be the most proactive partner and, in practice, the line between consultation and collaboration may be blurred.

Positioning the Service User in Research

The commitment to give the service user a 'voice' and an active role in research has led to a discernible shift in the positioning of the service user in health and social care research. Box 8.3 shows a typology of service user participation based upon a continuum from the user as passive research subject to research participant to research adviser to researcher commissioner and ultimately to user-controlled research.

Box 8.3 A Typology of service user participation		
Typology	**Role of service user**	**Indicative characteristics of each type**
Passive participation	Research subject	Service user participates by completing a questionnaire with fixed response boxes to tick *or* Data about service user is extracted from a pre-existing record
Participation by consultation	Research participant	Service user participates by taking part in a semi-structured interview or focus group
Participation by active research	Researcher	Service user plays an active part in the design of the research. This may include: development of data collection instruments; recruitment of participants and/or collection of data from them; dissemination of findings
Participation by research consultancy	Research consultant/ buddy	Service user is part of the research steering group and/or monitoring of research
Participation by research commissioning	Member of research committee	Service user is part of a research committee that commissions research and allocates funds
User-controlled research	Key member of steering group	Service user initiates and guides the research throughout

There is, of course, some overlap between the above categories. For example, both research consultants and researchers may well have input into research design. And a committee that monitors the progress of the research may well be the same committee as that which allocates funds. It is also possible for a service user to have multiple roles such as being involved in carrying out the research and acting as a research consultant.

8.3   CASE STUDIES

Service User as Research Subject

> **Case Study:**
> **Service user as research subject**
>
> A health services researcher was asked to conduct research about admissions to an in-patient mental health ward. The idea for this research came from the researcher working with senior management of a health trust. The aim was to find out whether there was variation in outcome according to who was conducting assessments, what time of day and where they took place, and the symptoms presented by the patient as well as their assessed level of risk. Data were collected from patient notes and an on-line database to construct an anonymous data file for statistical analysis. The analysis showed that the experience and professional background of who was doing the emergency assessment had a far larger effect on the outcome than features relating to the patient. This evidence was then used to underpin a major change in the organisation of emergency assessments to achieve lower rates of hospital admission.

> ☐ What was the input of service users in this research?
> ☐ What was the aim of this research and whose needs did it serve?
> ☐ Did this research improve the quality of care from the service user perspective?

In this example, the research subject was completely passive and had no involvement whatsoever in research. The results led to service change but this change was very much linked into, and guided by, needs of management to reduce in-patient admissions. Whether the changes were welcomed by the service user was not known. It is quite possible that the consequences of this research, which resulted in reduced hospital admission, would have been strongly opposed by service users and seen as a deterioration in the quality of care. Had the service users been involved as proactive partners the research would have identified the competing needs of all the stakeholders.

Service User as Research Participant

Case Study:
Service user as research participant

Research was set up to examine the psycho-social impact of an HIV-positive diagnosis. The interview schedule was devised by the two researchers on the project, neither of whom was HIV tested nor thought it very likely that they were HIV-positive. The interviews were lengthy and discussed intimate details of the participants' lives, such as receiving an HIV-positive diagnosis, disclosing HIV status to others, impact on sexual behaviour and interpersonal relationships. The precise content of the interviews was not fixed and the participants were encouraged to talk about what they felt was important to them regarding their HIV diagnosis. The research findings were published in peer-related journals and formed the basis of a book.

☑ What was the input of service users in this research?
☑ What could more active user involvement have added to the data collection?
☑ Is this research likely to have improved the quality of care from the service user perspective?

More active service user involvement could have collected more relevant data. The rapport that was established with some participants was substantial. However, one research participant said, 'Speaking to someone with the virus [HIV] you can let out exactly how you feel because you know they'll feel the same way' (see Green, 1998). The implication is that this rapport with someone not known to be HIV-positive would not be achieved. Nevertheless, the results provided an informed view of what it was like to be HIV-positive from the perspective of someone who was not. The results produced no discernible change in services.

Service User as Researcher

- What was the input of service users in this research?
- What were the pros and cons of active service user involvement?
- Is this research likely to have improved the quality of care from the service user perspective?

In this example the involvement of service users was key to the successful collection of data. Their role was instrumental in setting the agenda and collecting the data. However, their involvement had a cost, in that training was required and there were occasional mishaps with the tape recorder. The findings were well received by other researchers and a presentation describing the project was recognized by a national research network. The improvements that were identified were acted upon.

Service User as Research Consultant

A number of projects have used service users as expert consultants to ensure that the research is useful and meaningful. This type of service user involvement can be a challenge if the research is in areas requiring knowledge of highly specific academic areas often accompanied by technical language. The Buddy Programme described below aims to overcome such problems.

Case Study:
Service user as research consultant

The Buddy Programme developed by the Multiple Sclerosis (MS) Society (see www.mssociety.org) aims to improve communication about research, make research more accessible to the wider MS community and to encourage partnership working between researchers and people affected by MS. In this system, which is still in its infancy, a Buddy team of people with MS is allocated to every MS Society-funded research project. Buddies help communicate the research results to people affected by MS and they also inform the researchers about their experiences in living with MS so that the researchers learn to communicate more effectively with a lay audience.

- What is the main contribution of the Buddy?
- Does it matter that they are not experts in the research area?

In this system the Buddy is an important part of the research team. They play a key communication role by letting the researchers know what is important to, and how to communicate clearly with, people with MS. This emphasis on communication rather than carrying out the research means that expert knowledge of the research area is not required.

Service User as Research Commissioner

Increasingly, service users are becoming involved in research funding decisions and a number of mechanisms have been set up to facilitate this. Service user representation is common on Research & Development Groups in NHS Trusts. Such groups play a key a role in determining which research should or should not proceed, and may also have a budget to allocate. Disadvantages of having a sole service user member on this type of committee is that the service user may feel isolated and unsupported, sometimes even overwhelmed. Such representation is sometimes criticised as being tokenism. For this reason, more innovative and radical methods for service user involvement in commissioning research have been developed by many voluntary agencies.

> **Case Study:**
> **Service User as a commissioner of research**
>
> The MS Society have developed a Research Network of people with MS and their carers and this network plays an integral role in developing an overall research strategy and assessing research proposals. People from the Research Network take part in the Board that makes recommendations on the development and implementation of the overall research strategy. In addition, all applications for research funds are reviewed by a group that, as well as research experts, includes members of the Research Network. Applicants who fail to describe their research in a way that is accessible to a lay audience are unlikely to be successful.

 How is tokenism avoided in the above example?

Service user involvement on committees can be tokenistic and the service user can feel isolated. In the above example this is largely avoided by ensuring that service users have decision-making power. They have sufficient representation on decision-making committees to ensure that their vote makes a difference.

User-Controlled Research

Many service user organisations have R&D departments that carry out user-controlled research.

> **Case Study:**
> **User-controlled research**
>
> Age Concern research services conducted a survey about the lives, needs and issues of the over-50 population in the UK (for further information contact research@ace.org.uk). More than 1500 people across the UK were interviewed and the subsequent report provides intelligence for all agencies and companies involved in planning, developing or delivering products and services to the 50+ population, as well as to government departments, academics and voluntary organisations. The report can be purchased and Age Concern offer bespoke
>
> *(Continued)*

(Continued)

analysis of the data. The data collected thus is a source of funding for Age Concern and provides meaningful insight and intelligence about the 50+ population to assist those wishing to provide support to older people in the UK.

 ⏰ What advantages does this approach have for service users?

In this example there are many benefits for the service user. The service user decides on the content of the research and the results are used to generate income for the service user organisation and to assist the development of initiatives designed to support the service user.

8.4 ESTABLISHING EFFECTIVE ENGAGEMENT

Pros and Cons of Different Approaches

The examples of service user involvement in research described above show that there are both advantages and disadvantages. These are set out in Box 8.4.

Box 8.4 Stages of research and pros and cons of service user involvement		
	Pros	**Cons**
Commissioning research	Research relevant to service user needs	Researchers may make service user involvement tokenistic
Research design	Takes account of service user perspective	Service user may need technical training
Recruiting participants	Service user less threatening to other service users	There may be issues relating to confidentiality
Collecting data	Service user likely to have better rapport with other service users	Service user may be overly engaged without appropriate training
		(Continued)

(Continued)		
	Pros	**Cons**
Analysing data	Service user perspective may add new insight	Service user may lack the technical expertise
Disseminating results	Service user as a presenter 'roots' the research in real life	Audiences hear the service user not the research
Service change	Service user involvement lends the research greater credibilty	Service user only represents a particular stakeholder in the organisation
Impact of research on the service user	Involvement in research may be empowering	Involvement in research may be disturbing

Service user involvement is likely to result in more feasible and relevant research that takes account of what is important to service users and what is the best way to collect data from them. Service users have been used extensively to assist in the development of data collection instruments as they have a much clearer idea about what type of questions will strike a chord with other service users as well as which type of questions may cause offence. Service users have played a very effective role recruiting others to take part in research and interviewing them. Analysing and writing up data may require technical expertise that service users may not have but their input can help to make the report more meaningful to others. In addition, service users can play a key role in the dissemination of results. Service users' contributions at research conferences are invariably enlightening and powerful. Service users thus play a key role in ensuring that research is relevant to the service users. What we have also seen from the examples in section 8.2 is that research that does not involve service users is unlikely to result in a change in practice that is welcomed by service users.

There are also some potential disadvantages. The service user may lack technical research expertise and require training and this will increase the costs of the research. If the research is local and conducted with a specific service user group then confidentiality issues may arise as the service user acting as a researcher may be known to the participants. The impact of research activity upon the service user can also create problems. Whilst the evidence suggests that service users find active collaboration in research beneficial, it is possible that they will find the experience unrewarding.

Where the service user is positioned is crucial. If they are too passive they can be disempowered. If they are too active the research can be distorted by a particular individual personal agenda and idiosyncratic experiences. There are many examples that illustrate that service users can be very effective and in our experience the advantages of service user involvement clearly outweigh the disadvantages.

It is very easy for service user involvement to be passive and tokenistic and the practitioner researcher therefore needs to think carefully about how to establish active engagement. The following section looks at the basic infrastructure that is required to facilitate effective service user involvement in practice research.

Basic Building Blocks

Service user involvement in research is still in its infancy and few organisations have developed robust structures to facilitate it.

Most practitioner researchers will find that they will need to be proactive to generate service user engagement. Key ingredients for successful service user involvement are:

- Mutual respect and partnership
- Organisational support
- Time
- Financial support
- Training

Mutual respect and partnership is essential to a successful service user/ practitioner researcher collaboration. In many respects active service user involvement in research may help to foster such a relationship in that both the practitioner researcher and the service user will be involved in a joint endeavour where the carer/client division will be both less distinct and less meaningful.

Support from senior management is required to provide the infrastructure to facilitate service user involvement. Increasingly public sector organisations are developing systems to ensure that the service user voice is included in the development of services. Some organisations have advice and guidance about how to involve service users in research and this can be invaluable.

Practitioner research is often carried out with no budget and limited time. Funding may not stretch to providing training to service users about how to conduct interviews, or to pay them expenses for their participation. In this scenario an action research approach to engage service users has a number of advantages. Focus groups with service users may be used both to steer the research and to collect data to analyse. The service user thus becomes a research participant, an active researcher and a research consultant. This approach may facilitate a shift from passive service user involvement to a more genuine collaboration. It also need not be very resource-intensive.

Looking at the basic building blocks for service user involvement in research, it is apparent that many of the issues that arise parallel issues that confront the practitioner researcher. Few practitioner researchers or service users enjoy the luxury of being employed full time as a researcher and therefore time is at a premium. For many practitioner researchers and service users doing research is unlikely to be their main activity and they may have a number of training needs before they can embark on research. Nor is either likely to be successful without infrastructural support from the organisation in which the research is being carried out.

Taking Account of the Specific Needs of Service Users

Service users have by definition specific needs and the practitioner researcher needs to take account of these. If, for example, the service user has a long-term condition such as severe mental illness or coronary heart disease, they may have periods when they are not well enough to engage in any type of research activity and these periods may be relatively lengthy and unpredictable.

Collaborative research with service users with learning disabilities or mental impairment such as dementia presents a range of issues to resolve. Whilst these service users have views that need to inform the research process, they may not be able to articulate their views. The most common strategy used to address this is the substitution of service users with their carers or other significant others. The latter become, at least in theory, the advocates or voice of the service user. It is recognised that a carer may not know what the service user's view is or may not wish to express it, but they are generally regarded as being able to offer the closest approximation of it.

8.5 OWNERSHIP OF RESEARCH CONDUCTED IN COLLABORATION WITH SERVICE USERS

It is clear that without genuine collaboration with the service user research is unlikely to be a vehicle for change. At best, any research done without full consultation with the independent voice of the service user will result in a change that is beneficial to the manager or the practitioner. However, ceding ownership of research to the service user is a challenge, as the example in the next case study shows.

Case Study:
The complexity of ceding ownership

A project was jointly commissioned by a Strategic Health Authority (SHA), Primary Care Trust (PCT) and MIND. In addition, other service user and voluntary groups were involved in the project management group. The work was driven from different directions, with users seeking to improve services, the SHA trying to meet government targets and the PCT having the local lead for mental health. The service users were involved at all levels since MIND is a user organisation. Other service users were involved in discussing their own case studies for analysis within the research. The practitioner researcher on the project coordinated the design, delivery and presentation of the work in its entirety from ethics, to interview, to transcribing and on-stage presentation. The research served to bring together diverse opinion and positions into one document from which the commissioners could host a series of forums. A number of changes emerged as a result of the work, including the appointment of a project officer.

The project produced an interesting dilemma. The issue concerned the provision of day services. Service users were quite clear that what was needed was a 'bricks and mortar' building to house day services, whereas health care professionals argued that what was required were peripatetic day services that could travel around the district 'lodging' in public buildings, such as village halls, throughout the week. Research and experience elsewhere suggest that the latter is more cost-effective. Not surprisingly therefore, this suggestion was adopted.

☐ To what extent was this research collaborative?
☐ Whose interests were served?

This project succeeded to a large extent in collaborative involvement with service users and also created changes of benefit to service users. However, the most significant change took less notice of the service users' voice than those of health care professionals and management. This illustrates how service user involvement can so easily slide into tokenism. It also raises the question that if practitioner researchers are going to collaborate with service users and then ignore their views, why should service users want to get involved in the future.

SUMMARY

- Service users have a key role to play in practitioner research and research done without their involvement has major limitations when it is applied in practice
- There are various styles of engagement (consultation, collaboration and user-led). Without a genuine collaboration with service users the practitioner researcher will not be able to use the research to drive change in practice that will be accepted by the service users
- To use research to improve practice it is imperative that ownership of research is shared and conducted as a mutual endeavour. Compared to the traditional research paradigm that uses service users as research subjects, this involves ceding control to the service user
- Without such control involvement of service users will not be more than tokenistic

FURTHER READING

Beresford, P. (2002) 'User involvement in research and evaluation: liberation or regulation?', *Social Policy and Society*, 1 (2): 93–103

Peter Beresford has written many articles about service user involvement in research. He shows how involvement can easily become tokenistic.

Faulkner, A. and Thomas, P. (2002) 'User-led research and evidence based medicine.' *British Journal of Psychiatry* 180: 1–3

Alison Faulkner has written a number of articles looking at why user-led research is important and the role it plays in evidence-based practice and the development of mental health services.

9
Writing the Research Report

This chapter is concerned with how practitioner researchers present their research. The process of translating research practice into readable text, in whatever form, is far from straightforward. It is time-consuming and challenges the practitioner researcher cognitively and ethically. However, it is a process that is essential to ensure that practitioner research becomes recognised as research that makes a difference to the way professionals practise in education, health and social care services.

This chapter will focus on:

⇒   Writing as part of the research process
⇒   Writing up the research report
⇒   Establishing integrity and balance
⇒   Disseminating the report

9.1 WRITING AS PART OF THE RESEARCH PROCESS

In an ideal world the cycle outlined in Figure 9.1 would be a systematic process and completed whenever a piece of research was undertaken. However, practitioner researchers in the real world often encounter barriers and hurdles that must be overcome.

In the cycle described in Figure 9.1 the practitioner researcher undertakes research (a) and writes a report (b) based on the work; this report is then disseminated (c). In practice, the process becomes hampered: for example, the work of the practitioner researcher changes and the formal preparation

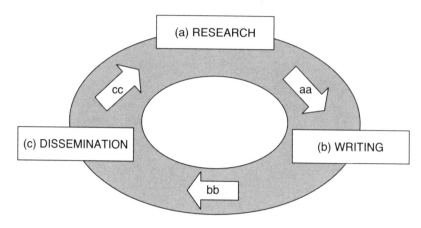

FIGURE 9.1 *A cycle of research dissemination*

of a report is lost (aa); the report is not well received and dissemination is actively or passively hampered (bb); the report is written and well received, but is not made available for others to use in further research (cc).

Practitioner researchers should endeavour to complete this loop in order that they may generate a knowledge base of good quality practitioner research. The development and collation of such a body of knowledge is essential if practitioner research is to be recognised as a significant research tradition.

9.2 WRITING UP THE RESEARCH

Practitioner researchers often view writing up the research as the end of a long and arduous journey. The process of writing up, however, should not be at the end of the research; it should be under construction throughout the research. There are many ways to achieve this.

The Research Diary

The research diary, or research portfolio, is a journal that practitioner researchers keep in which to detail their involvement in the research. The use of the diary as a process internal to the research study is valuable; it forms a record to which the researcher can return in order to re-contextualise decisions made about the study. This may also form part of the audit trail by which the basis of decisions at each stage of the process can be surfaced (Lincoln and Guba, 1985). The diary is a comprehensive record of the research process and contains a reflection on that process. Maintaining a research diary provides the practitioner researcher with a record of both the research process and his or her own development as a practitioner researcher.

The research diary is a means of planning and keeping the research on track. In quantitative research the diary might be used to note down data and data analysis procedures, for example, useful statistical tests and their interpretation. In action research the diary might be used to monitor progress through the action cycle: for example, key indicators by which the group demonstrated readiness to change. In qualitative research the diary might be used to explore the reflexive relationship between the research and the researcher: for example, the impact of the researcher's perception of a particular interviewee and the problems this created with that interview.

The diary also contributes to the development of the practitioner researcher and is a record of his or her developing research experience. The research diary may record different types of experiences:

- Running descriptions: specific concrete descriptions of events, conversations
- Recall of forgotten material: issues, problems and thoughts that are recalled out of context
- Interpretative notes: notes offering an analysis of a situation and the impact of that analysis on the perception of the research
- Personal impressions and feelings: subjective reactions to issues arising from the research
- Reminders to look for additional information or follow up a lead

Memory is selective and a research diary should be recorded regularly and promptly after significant events. The longer the delay the greater the likelihood that what is remembered will only be that which fits within existing schema. The practitioner researcher should develop a system for capturing research experiences as clearly as possible. Records made 'on the spot' during the research can act as 'memory sparkers' that remind the practitioner researcher of thoughts and feelings at the time. These jottings can subsequently be expanded and clarified. Practitioner researchers can also share this record with their research supervisor and use it to track research supervision (see Chapter 11).

Box 9.1   Keeping a research diary

- The diary is personal. There is no right or wrong way of keeping it. Write what is important to you
- Write it as it is, not as you think it should be
- Treat it as a friend that you can use, not an imposition to be done

(Continued)

(Continued)

- Write, write, write – say what you want to. Don't censor yourself
- Use diagrams, pictures or any other means of expressing yourself
- Use it as a workbook – don't be afraid of revising entries and highlighting things
- Don't be rigid about how you keep the diary. Be able to change the format if it is helpful
- Stick at it
- If you talk to someone about what you have written (e.g. your research supervisor), feel free to reflect/write on this conversation too
- Be selective – don't write everything down

(with acknowledgement to Walker, 1994)

Writing up During the Research

It would be remarkable for a practitioner researcher to complete a piece of research and write a report from beginning to end in one sitting. It is usually a more inconsistent process. This can be beneficial because it enables the practitioner researcher to engage with the research from different perspectives.

Practitioner researchers may find themselves obliged to write up some of the work whilst it is ongoing. Research governance often requires the submission of interim reports to ensure that the research is being carried out in accordance with the research proposal. Students may also be required to submit drafts of work to supervisors during a period of academic study involving research.

The error that many practitioner researchers make is to assume that they have nothing to write before they have completed the research. Regardless of the type of research, there are discrete phases that can be written up. It should not be assumed that, because a particular phase of the work has been written down, it is a completed piece of work. Each piece, when brought together within the full report, will need to be revised on several occasions to ensure it is consistent and readable. However, it is far easier to revise a manuscript than a blank sheet of paper.

Writing up while the research is in progress is an opportunity for the practitioner researcher to practise sustained writing. This can be psychologically draining and time-consuming. An analogy can be made with a marathon; training is essential if the writer is not going to collapse half way through the work. Effort is required to develop different aspects of writing. First, the practitioner researcher needs to organise a comfortable, ergonomic workspace and practise the physical act of sitting at a word processor for a long period of time. Secondly, effort is required to develop sustained concentration, which is difficult in the real world of multiple distractions. Thirdly, the practitioner researcher must practise the psychological manipulation of words, sentences and paragraphs into a meaningful text. Lastly, effort is required to grasp and organise complex concepts surrounding the research. This might include the research design, participants and the context. It might also include the practitioner researcher's own relationship and engagement with the research, the basis of which might be notes recorded in the research diary. Writing up in progress is a way of capturing the personal meanings associated with the study as the basis for later reports: 'Leaving all the writing to the end is to risk losing these learnings' (McLeod, 2003: 27).

Writing up in progress is an opportunity for the researcher to experiment with different voices. These voices will be addressed in detail below, but essentially the researcher must decide whose story is being told by the research. It may take some time before the writer is confident that the story can be told from a particular perspective with accuracy, trustworthiness and sensitivity. Sharing work-in-progress early on with colleagues or a research supervisor is a useful way of avoiding substantial re-writes later on.

The Purpose and Process of Writing Up Research

The purpose of writing up a research report is to disseminate the findings of the research. Writing up the report demonstrates ownership and responsibility for the study. It is the practitioner researcher who will receive the *kudos* associated with the study, but who also has to take responsibility for what was done.

The report should demonstrate that the practitioner researcher understands relevant material concerning both the subject and method of the research. The practitioner researcher, drawing on practice knowledge, will be able to give a good account of the subject of the research. This understanding will enable limitations of current knowledge and the importance of strengthening such deficient areas of practice to be highlighted.

Practitioner researchers often become disillusioned that the small-scale work they have undertaken does not immediately have a significant impact upon practice locally and nationally. However, the skill to be demonstrated here is to present original material that motivates others to develop the ideas into further research. The practitioner researcher should develop an understanding of how the study fits into the current world-view, by addressing:

- What does this study add to current understanding?
- How does it link to what is already known?
- Where does it contradict or conflict with what is known?

If the research is to achieve appropriate recognition, the practitioner researcher must clearly demonstrate what it contributes to the current understanding of the topic. This is at least partly due to how the practitioner researcher presents the research. Writing a report that is articulate is a skill that is easily overlooked, particularly for the hard-pressed practitioner researcher. However, writing that is confused, rambling or unnecessarily dense so often reveals unclear thinking (Morse, 1991). The report that is overly complex and full of jargon antagonises readers and makes them less receptive to its contents. Preparing a report that is clear and articulate maximises the possibility that the research will, at least, be read.

Time and Space

From a practical perspective writing up is time-consuming (see also section 7.4). It requires significant and sustained effort that would be psychologically draining even were it to be possible for the practitioner researcher to identify the necessary time. Different stages of writing the report will require access to different resources. So, to complete the literature review the practitioner researcher will need access to virtual or real texts. For the analysis, access will be required to computer time and thinking time.

A significant task for practitioner researchers is to balance the practitioner and researcher components of their role. Robson (2002) notes the difficulty of trying to undertake research in addition to normal commitments. This balance may be a cause of stress within the role, with the practitioner researcher left feeling that neither the role of practitioner nor the role of researcher is effectively fulfilled.

Constraints on available time may be highlighted, particularly when preparing the research report. In order to write effectively and efficiently many practitioner researchers will need time to settle into their writing. Trying to engage in writing in short bursts is usually ineffective. The time required to write up research is consistently and universally longer than anticipated by the practitioner researcher; writing up generally takes as long as the rest of the research processes put together. Many see this as the least rewarding stage of the research process. The excitement of designing and delivering the study are complete and the systematic documentation of the study becomes a chore.

In order to write in a manner that is both economical and effective, practitioner researchers should build in thinking time. McLeod (2003) suggests that practitioner researchers, particularly those coming to research through academic study, become blocked and anxious when faced with writing a research report. Completion of the 'operational' phase of the study only means that the practical and external tasks have been completed. Writing a report that merely reports the successful completion of tasks can only ever be shallow and descriptive. The practitioner researcher needs the space to think about what he or she has found and to begin to put those findings within the context of practice.

McLeod (2003: 36) offers some 'Suggestions for easing the pain of writing', which practitioner researchers may find helpful. However, finding time and space for writing the report is always problematic. It is a time too, when there is limited visible evidence of research occurring, when those who have a call on the practitioner researcher's time feel able to disturb or interrupt the flow of work. Paradoxically, this is the time when the practitioner researcher most needs space and time to make sense of his or her research activities: 'Get it known and respected that you are not available for discussion, or whatever, at that time' (Robson, 2002: 520).

9.3 ESTABLISHING INTEGRITY AND BALANCE

In simplistic terms practitioner researchers write research reports in order to accurately recount the structure, process and outcome of their research. In doing so the work that has been undertaken is made accessible to others. However, getting from research activity to research report is a complex process. Problems lie within assumptions about how the practitioner researcher accurately recounts the research process. Practitioner researchers have to decide how they will handle issues that may have arisen through the research; the root of this dilemma is in establishing integrity and balance within the report.

Case Study:
Joan – integrity and balance as sources of prevarication

Joan is a practitioner research who has recently undertaken research within her own field of practice. She commenced the work through personal interest rather than academic study. However, as research is part of her role, her NHS Trust has provided her with access to an experienced research supervisor. Joan's research examined how the attitudes of the health care professional impacted upon the behaviour and experience of service users with a history of self-harm. Joan used a participatory action research design for the work. She found the design challenging, but stimulating, as it opened up areas of the research that she had not foreseen.

Data have been collected and Joan has only to write the report in order to complete the project. However, Joan does not seem able to find the time or the energy to complete the work. She prevaricates, writes and re-writes the literature review and design sections.

(Continued)

(*Continued*)

Joan and her supervisor hold a crisis meeting. Joan explores what is happening in her life at present; this includes marital disharmony, school problems for her children and lack of security at work due to service reorganisation. Joan's supervisor recognises these issues, but focuses on the work she has been undertaking and challenges Joan about her findings. Joan acknowledges that she is distressed by her findings. In exploring this distress Joan indicates that her findings suggest a link between the attitude of health care professionals and service user behaviour. This, in itself, is unsurprising, but Joan is concerned with the anger expressed by service user participants about the issue. She feels that if her research is put in the public domain:

- It will reflect badly on her colleagues who are also her friends
- It will reflect badly on the Trust and 'heads will roll'
- Service user organisations will use it to attack the service in which she works

Joan's case study presents a number of issues that practitioner researchers may encounter when writing up practitioner research. In writing the report the practitioner researcher has to make decisions about voice, reflexivity and textual representation. These represent three engaging, but painful issues (Lincoln and Guba, 2003):

- In whose voice should the report appear?
- What is the relationship between the researcher and the research?
- How does the research identify and represent on paper the essence of the study?

Voice

Finding 'voice' for the study is a hurdle that all researchers must overcome, but for practitioner researchers the voice may be less clear than for others. This is the nature of the insider's, rather than outsider's, engagement and relationship with the field. The 'voice' to which reference is made is the voice that speaks through the research report. This may be, for example, the voice of the research commissioner, the researcher or the participants (Robson, 2002). These voices will not tell the same story; one voice will come to dominate the research report.

Case Study:
Joan *(continued)* – integrity and balance in presentation

Joan's data includes the experience of service users who have self-harmed in in-patient facilities. She struggles with how to present this type of data and tries four different approaches to the same participant's report:

(*Continued*)

(Continued)

1 "Service users reported that nurses were helpful and attended to basic needs. However, they found difficulty in appreciating the underlying and precipitating features of the event"
2 "Service users recounted instances to the researcher where nurses verbalised negative judgements about service users who deliberately cut themselves. Attention was given to the physical needs, but not to the associated psychosocial needs"
3 "Chris (Interviewee 4 pseudonym) reported to the researcher that he had experienced overtly hostile responses from the nurse to whom he spoke. This response increased Chris's feelings of guilt and shame. The nurse did attend to basic needs (cleaning and dressing), but this only lowered his already damaged self-esteem"
4 "I showed the nurse where I had, you know, cut and she just looked at me angrily and said "Oh, that's bloody typical of you and all I need right now." She gave me some bandages and helped me to clean it up. She was OK then, but I just knew she didn't understand, how could she, she wasn't where I was. It made me feel horrible; a complete failure".

The examples presented above progress from an objective report, that attempts to eliminate the subjective experience, to a direct report which simply permits the reader to make their own sense of the participant's experience. Practitioner researchers must find the right voice in which to present the work. They must be content that this voice represents the essence of the study. Two factors will influence/affect the choice of voice (see Figure 9.2).

* The type of research that the practitioner researcher has undertaken. Here distinction can be drawn between research that is located in the objective world, social world or individually constructed world (see Chapter 1). If the practitioner researcher uses an objective voice in a research report located in the individually constructed world, the participants' experience will not be represented.
* The purpose of the report. For some audiences a third person 'scientific voice' is required in order to give the report credibility. For others, the intensity of the first person is essential in order to maximise impact and change attitudes.

Once the work is in the public domain it is impossible for the practitioner researcher to retrieve it and, consequently, the decision about voice should not be taken lightly. Fine et al. (2000) suggest that the social researcher should strive to write a report that truly represents the voice of those who trusted the researcher enough to share their opinions. This can be facilitated by addressing the questions in Box 9.2.

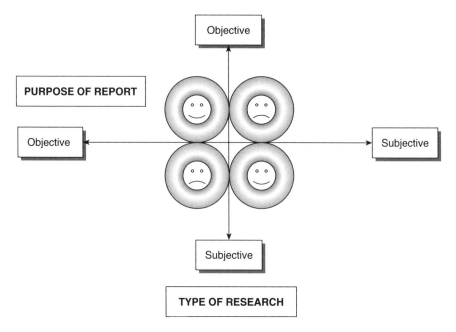

FIGURE 9.2   *A continuum of voice*

Box 9.2   Questions to assist in finding voice

- Have I connected the 'voices' and 'stories' of individuals back to the set of historic, structural and economic relations in which they are situated?
- Have I deployed multiple methods so that very different kinds of analyses can be constructed?
- Have I described the mundane?
- Have some informants/constituencies/participants reviewed the material with me and interpreted, dissented, challenged my interpretations? And then how do I report these departures/agreements in perspective?
- How far do I want to go with respect of theorising the words of the informants?
- Have I considered how these data could be used for progressive, conservative, repressive social policies?
- Where have I backed into the passive voice and decoupled my responsibility for my interpretations?
- Who am I afraid will see these analyses? Who is rendered vulnerable/responsible or exposed by these analyses? Am I willing to show him/her/them the text before publication? If not, why not? Could I publish his/her/their comments as an epilogue? What's the fear?
- What dreams am I having about the material presented?

(Continued)

(Continued)

■ To what extent has my analysis offered an alternative to the 'commonsense' or dominant discourse? What challenges might very different audiences pose to the analysis presented?

(Fine et al., 2000: 126)

Reflexivity

The relationship between the researcher and the research is reflexive. As Figure 9.3 illustrates, the researcher and research affect each other.

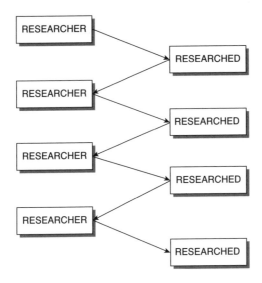

FIGURE 9.3 *Reflexivity during research*

Reflexivity means that at every stage of the research process the practitioner researcher has influenced, consciously or unconsciously, the process and has been influenced in turn by the research process. For example:

- Joan's personal interest and experience of self-harm has stimulated interest in researching the subject
- Reading around the topic has shaped her thinking about her practice
- The sense she has made of her reading has been shaped by her unique experience and understanding of practical work with this service user group
- Decisions about the form of the research have been shaped by others' research in the field

- Joan contemplates the most suitable method based on her experience of service users with whom she has worked
- And so on

Reflexivity is present throughout the research process and practitioner researchers should be conscious of its presence (see also section 11.4). However, they may find the concept problematic and acknowledging the influence of reflexivity may fluctuate throughout the life of the study. Practitioner researchers should habitually stand back from their activities and examine reflexivity at each stage of decision-making in relation to the operation of the research. The research diary may be a helpful way of assisting the researcher to stand back from the research.

Reflexivity is also part of the dissemination process. It is a process between the researcher and the imaginary audience (see Figure 9.4). This can be a virtual process where practitioner researchers puts themselves in the shoes of the readers. It can also be a real process where the practitioner researcher asks colleagues to read and comment on drafts of the report. Joan's fantasies about the reaction of her 'audience' to her findings impact upon her thinking about the construction of the final report. In order to eliminate the potential threat of a bad audience response, Joan contemplates an objective, neutralised report. However, she is conscious that such a report would not be an accurate or truthful representation of the information with which participants trusted her to report.

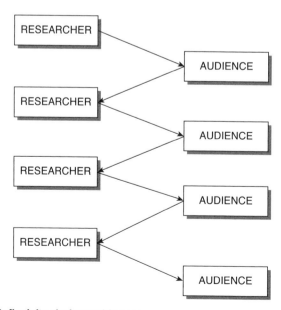

FIGURE 9.4   *Reflexivity during writing up*

Textual Representation

In writing reports that practitioner researchers believe to be authentic, they must wrestle with two problems, identified by Lincoln and Guba (2003) as crises of authority and representation.

The crisis of authority concerns the authority of practitioner researchers to define the researched world through their research. Research reports implicitly argue that a named aspect of the world has been studied and its portrayal, on the written page, is how it is. Such arrogance may not be intentional, but is implicit. Associated with this is the unintentional simplifying of the world. It is not possible to express the complexity of a given topic within a single piece of work; however, there is a risk that it will read as a definitive account.

The crisis in representation focuses on the group of research participants though this is not, as might appear, an issue of sampling. The problem lies in a group speaking on behalf of a wider group of individuals, all of whom possess a unique view of the research issue. Once a report has been written and disseminated the accounts can become the accounts of all people encompassed within this field of study. The practitioner researcher creates a world that is effectively defined by the shared experience expressed in the research report. This may silence those whose experience is not in accord with that documented.

In the case study outlined earlier in this chapter Joan was attempting to authentically represent the voice of the service user. In order to do this Joan should consider what it is she can say about the world of this particular service user group. A report that generalises the experience of the group implies that the work defines the parameters of the service user experience. Similarly, others who engage in self-harming behaviour may read a generalised report. These readers may be excluded because the report, which purports to define a complex phenomenon, does not encompass their experience.

 How should Joan accurately represent the experience of the informants of her study? Accurately reporting all data can be hazardous for the practitioner researcher, both from the perspective of an abdication of responsibility to present a balanced report, but also in terms of dealing with the consequences of challenging institutional power bases (McNiff, 2002).

☐ How should Joan encompass complexity and avoid presenting a single view of the world?
☐ How should Joan maintain responsibility for the study and faithfully represent the respondents' views?

9.4   DISSEMINATION

Reports of practitioner research should be placed within the public domain. There is a reasonable expectation that anyone who submits work for publication in any form of journal should, at a very basic level, be able to:

- Write articulately
- Argue coherently
- Present work that is logical
- Work within given time scales
- Undertake accurate referencing

However, these very basic skills are so often missing. Articles that are submitted to journals may be incomplete, incoherent and inaccurately referenced. Reviewing such reports is inevitably influenced by the struggle of reviewers to make sense of what they are reading. When these papers are subsequently returned for basic amendment, regardless of the quality of the content, authors become fractious and disheartened. Paying attention, at the outset, to the basics of presentation and enlisting the aid of friends and colleagues as critical readers can avoid distress for both the practitioner researcher and the reviewer.

Practitioner researchers, interested in disseminating the findings of research through publication, quickly come to recognise that the structure of the report varies significantly dependent on the aim. Box 9.3 compares and contrasts some of the different forms of publication in which practitioner researchers could consider disseminating their work.

In order to explore the publication process as a practical endeavour reference will be made to Joan's work referred to in the case study above.

Academic journal   Academic journals are primarily concerned with the publication of scholarly work. The audience may be considered to be familiar with the style of a standardised research report and able to connect the report to a theoretical understanding of the field. The structure of the report should, therefore, provide a comprehensive examination of design and method and place the findings in a theoretical context. Issues such as the Research Assessment Exercise (for both the individual and the higher education institution) and the current prevalent funding streams may influence the style and content seen as desirable by such journals.

Joan's report might highlight:

- A critical appraisal of the participatory action research model used as the design of the study
- The experience of working in participation with service users
- Critical appraisal of theoretical models of self-harming behaviour as a context for examining the research findings

Box 9.3 Forms of publication			
Orientation	**Aim**	**Interest**	**Context**
Academic journal	Scholarly activity	Design and method Underpinning theoretical constructs	Research Assessment Exercise (RAE) Funding streams
Professional journal	Development of professional practice	Professional status New practice	Political influence Influential and/or competing factions
In-house organisation reports	Organisational development	Service governance	Political influence CHAI/Ofsted reports
User report	Improve service user experience	Dissemination of good practice	New and emerging issues

Professional journal   The professional journal is interested in professional development issues. A professional audience should be considered as peers or colleagues within the workplace. This audience is primarily uni-professional or within a specialist field of practice, though it is noted that a number of multi-professional journals are now appearing. This group will be less familiar with reading research reports, though they are an increasingly informed audience. Interest may be in the rich description of field issues that might enable the audience to connect with their own field of practice with a view to transferability (Lincoln and Guba, 1985). The interest is often in how professionals can optimise the delivery of services to users. The prevailing political landscape and the activities of dominant pressure groups within such bodies may influence such journals.

Joan's report might highlight:

- The implications for current and future professional practice
- Evaluation of the contribution of the research to practice development
- Partnership between service users and health care professionals

In-house report   These publications are designed to be read by various organisation employees. The report might, therefore, focus on the implications of

the findings for the organisation/organisations as a whole. The current 'driver' from the government department/funding agency for the organisation may have a profound impact on the area of interest for such journals.
   Joan's report might highlight:

- The impact of the findings on current service provision
- Training and development issues emerging from the research
- How the findings can be used to address quality and governance issues

User journal   The service user report is a relatively new phenomenon and reflects the current drive to engage service users at all levels of health, social and education organisations (see also Chapter 8). Such journals may have a very diverse readership, including service users and service providers; for example, a report might be prepared for parents and children in a school. The report focus must be written with users in mind. The style should be uncomplicated by unnecessary jargon or terminology and the focus should place the findings in the context of the experience of service users.
Joan's report might highlight:

- How staff attitude impacts upon users' experience of the service and what users choose to share with professionals during assessment
- What users can do to limit the impact of staff attitude on their use of the service
- What services should do to improve staff attitude
- The experience of research partnership between health care professionals and service users

It is recognized that most journals provide specific guidance to authors in relation to preferred style and content.

SUMMARY
- Research is not completed until the work has been put in the public domain
- The research diary is an important tool that practitioner researchers can use to monitor the progress of the research and their own development as researchers
- Writing up is an on-going process and should not be left until the completion of the data collection and analysis
- Preparing a report that will be read should be the objective of the practitioner researcher. Research reports will not be read unless the writer has clearly presented and considered the contents of the report. Presenting a report that is clear and readable is a skill that practitioner researchers should develop

- Writing up research can create as many problems for practitioner researchers as carrying out the study. The practitioner researcher should consider at the outset who is being represented by the report
- Publication of research through various journals and reports will disseminate the work quickly and effectively. Preparing the right report for the right journal requires consideration prior to writing the report

FURTHER READING

Alvesson, M. and Sköldberg, K. (2000) *Reflexive Methodology.* **London: Sage**

This book examines how researchers can practise and write reflexively. Whilst it does not address issues of practitioner research directly, the discussion has wide applicability.

Fine, M., Weis, L., Weseen, S. and Wong, L. (2000) 'For whom? Qualitative research, representations and social responsibilities', in N. Denzin and Y. Lincoln (eds), *Handbook of Qualitative Research.* **Thousand Oaks, CA: Sage. pp. 107–31**

This chapter offers a commentary on the ways in which qualitative research can be presented. It critically reviews approaches that fail to serve the interests of the participants and exhorts the researcher to greater degrees of integrity.

10
Research Utilisation: Maximising the Impact of Research on Practice

There is a substantial body of research in the libraries of higher education institutions and health care Trusts that has not been accessed or used since it was placed there. Some of this research may be weak, non-contemporary or have insignificant findings, but there probably remains a core of good quality research that has never been utilised. Research that remains 'on the shelf' represent a significant wasted investment for the practitioner researcher, for the organisation and for participants.

The translation of research findings into practice is complex and impacts from the micro to the macro level of service delivery. It is as challenging for individual practitioners to change safe and familiar practice as it is for service managers to allocate budgets to new forms of practice. As we discussed in Chapter 3, practitioner researchers needs to be familiar with both 'research' and 'development' in order to maximise the impact of their research.

This chapter will discuss how practitioner researchers can build in strategies that will help to maximise the impact of their research. The chapter will focus on:

⇨ The context of research utilisation
⇨ Working collaboratively
⇨ Marketing research
⇨ Motivation to change
⇨ Change and learning organisations

10.1 THE CONTEXT OF RESEARCH UTILISATION

Research utilisation is the integration of research findings into practice. Practice, in this instance, may be considered at a micro/practitioner level through to a macro/organisational level. In Chapter 3 we discussed research designs that integrate change as part of the research process. There are several factors outside the control of the practitioner researcher that also need to be considered. Change brought about through research utilisation is complex, and Weiss (1986) has described seven different models by which the practitioner researcher can understand utilisation (see Box 10.1). Practitioner researchers often assume that, because research has been successfully completed, findings will automatically be adopted with a concomitant change in practice. Weiss describes this as the knowledge-driven model; other models may apply with less ideal outcomes for the practitioner researcher, which can be disheartening and demoralising.

Box 10.1   Weiss's seven models of research utilisation

- The **knowledge-driven** model: research is used to generate knowledge; this knowledge is then used to drive action in practice
- The **problem-solving** model: research is commissioned and undertaken in response to an identified problem
- The **interactive** model: researchers engage in a continuous process of interaction with stakeholders to generate research projects and throughout the research process
- The **political** model: research is only adopted if it is congruent with the current political landscape
- The **enlightenment** model: individual research studies make little difference; change occurs as a result of a constant stream of insights, knowledge and perspectives
- The **tactical** model: the research is less important than the fact that research is taking place, which is used as a tactic to deflect criticism or delay action
- The **intellectual enterprise** model: researchers and policy-makers are influenced by trends in popular thinking

---

Practitioner researchers need to give thought to how findings will be marketed to practitioners and managers alike (see Alan's case study below). Planning for impact at the start of the study will reduce the amount of research that remains on the library shelf. Practitioner researchers need to be independent and critical voices within the public services. However, the astute practitioner researcher will recognise that compromise and negotiation will help ensure that this critical voice is heard rather than being silenced or overwhelmed.

> **Case Study:**
> **Alan – community mental health services**
>
> A Mental Health NHS Trust was investing heavily in the development of a range of new services in the local community. These services were supported and encouraged by central government as international research suggested that these services were a means of increasing engagement with discharged service users.
>
> Alan, a practitioner researcher, undertook research with service users about planned discharge from hospital into these new services. The findings of this study suggested that the service users interviewed in the study were confused by the variety of new services that were being developed in the community. The service users reported considerable bewilderment about the purpose of the new services. They were unsure what services they would have access to and whether they could contact the services themselves or would have to be referred by their GP in the first instance.
>
> Alan's findings were critical of the current direction in which the Trust was being steered to invest; here Weiss's political model of research utilisation is relevant. The findings of the study were perceived by the Trust as challenging and Alan received very little support from the Trust to disseminate the findings, if not actual discouragement. However, a form of compromise was attained and utilisation supported. Alan's findings were used to suggest ways in which the current policy direction could be improved. The findings were presented as being critical of the 'signposting' of new services rather than the new services *per se*. Alan was commissioned to undertake further research to examine how signposting could be improved.

 At any particular time different models of research utilisation may be dominant depending on current 'live' issues and the subject of the research.

☐ Does Weiss's work help to explain the level of utilisation in past research projects within your workplace?

☐ How can practitioner researchers use Weiss's work to encourage research utilisation in their workplace?

10.2 WORKING COLLABORATIVELY

Collaborative research is a loose term used to describe research where two or more people work together on a single project. Chapter 8 outlined and discussed the many different approaches to collaborative working in relation to service users, many of which can be applied to collaboration with colleagues. Collaboration is currently seen as the direction in which practitioner research should be developed. For example, research collaboration between higher education institutions and industry, commerce, government and public sectors is actively promoted (Smith and Katz, 2000).

The UK Department of Health national health research strategy emphasises the involvement of different collaborative stakeholders in attaining its vision of improving the health of the nation through research (DoH, 2006).

Collaboration, however, is a term that has many meanings depending on the context in which it is being used. It may be used to include anyone who has had any involvement in the research, which has been described as 'weak collaboration'. This is akin to 'consultation' described in Chapter 8. It may also be used to refer only to those who have contributed directly to all the main research tasks over the duration of the project, which has been described as strong collaboration (Katz and Martin, 1997).

Case Study:
Mary and Michael – interprofessional collaboration or research assistance

A team of, primarily, medical doctors and nurses work closely within a practice area. Mary, the medical consultant, has a reputation for attracting research funding and coordinating large-scale trials of clinical procedures. In order for the latest study to be undertaken Mary needs qualitative data to be collected from service users. She invites Michael, a nurse practitioner researcher, to collaborate with her on the study to collect this data.

Michael is given a structured data collection instrument to complete with service users. He questions the appropriateness of the tool for the collection of good qualitative data. Mary tells him that she is in charge of the study and the qualitative data are not essential to the study. It is being collected to ensure that the study receives all the necessary governance approvals. However, she thought that Michael might like to do this work to give him some research practice and the opportunity for publication.

 There are many elements here that relate to the level of service user involvement in research discussed in Chapter 8.

  ☐ Who will benefit from this study and in what ways?
  ☐ Can Michael publish his work on the study as practitioner research?
  ☐ Can this study be described as collaborative research?

Collaboration provides the opportunity for practitioner researchers to be involved at different levels of the research. As such, the role of a research assistant may provide a useful opportunity for practitioner researchers to develop research and writing skills. In doing so, however, they should consider the ethical dimension of their involvement. For example, Michael, in the case study above, might wonder if the collection of qualitative data in such an arbitrary and superficial manner was disempowering to service users. Practitioner researchers involved in collaborations need to feel able to challenge assumptions about the world promulgated as 'truth' by others involved in the study (see the research worlds described in Chapter 1).

Similarly, practitioner researchers writing up research collaborations must assert their perspective. This may involve ensuring that the issues addressed in Chapter 9 – voice, reflexivity and textual representation – are embodied in the writing.

An alternative way of examining collaboration may be to think of it as a pair of intersecting continuums (see Box 10.2). On one arm of the continuum are the participants of the collaboration and on the other the focus of the collaboration.

Box 10.2   Modes of collaboration

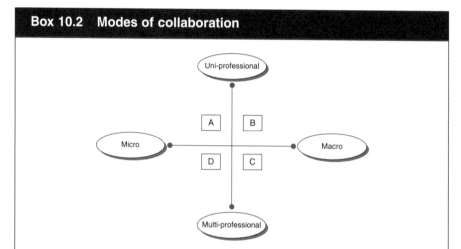

This model can be applied to research into the teaching of citizenship.

A: Two teachers develop a small-scale research project to examine how teaching styles impact on the development of citizenship within a single class year.
B: A group of teachers from different schools work together to develop a research project. The project examines how teaching styles impact on the development of citizenship within the first three years of secondary/senior school. The project collects a large volume of data from different schools and contexts. These data are compared and contrasted.
C: A school, a social services department and a regional police force work on a multi-armed project to examine how public services can work together to develop citizenship in young people.
D: A teacher, community police officer and social worker develop a participatory action research study to understand how children develop an awareness of citizenship.

Collaborative working should also encompass 'joined up' thinking. Engaging in joined up thinking avoids duplication of work undertaken by different agencies working in isolation. It also avoids single agencies thinking that they can solve large-scale social problems independently.

There are many similarities in the issues facing public services in the UK. If practitioner researchers simply address these problems in a micro/ uni-professional manner the findings can only relate to a small area of the problem and have limited impact. For example, current health policy encourages partnership between elements of health services, within which attention has focused on primary mental health care. In a single geographical area practitioner researchers may, separately, undertake studies that:

- Evaluate the links between a mental health trust and primary care
- Examine the links between a general practice and the independent mental health services
- Examine the experience of mental health service users in primary care

Each study, in isolation, may be of good quality and undertaken by practitioner researchers with the best intentions. It is, nonetheless, apparent that a single integrated study, incorporating common elements, would add significant value. Fragmented thinking in the separate studies would result in less efficient use of funding, practitioners and service users being over-researched and the findings disseminated to smaller, single agency, audiences. In joining up thinking, a single multi-agency study would promote efficient use of resources, reduce impact on those in the research field and ensure that a larger audience received the findings that could, in turn, work collaboratively on the recommendations.

Practitioner researchers undertaking projects collaboratively can engage in joined up thinking, which will enhance the quality of the research and outcomes as can be see in case study below. It is more cost-effective and avoids eroding the goodwill of practitioner and service users by continually researching them.

Case Study:
Health needs assessment

A practitioner researcher was involved in a 'health impact assessment on a new housing development'. The work involved collaboration between the borough council, a Primary Care NHS Trust and an NHS Health Authority.

The project was highly successful and the findings were well regarded. However, the practitioner researcher, as project coordinator, had to surmount a number of problems throughout the life of the study. For example:

- Coordinating and establishing meetings and feedback from the management team
- Coordinating consensus between diverse views and perceptions of problems and issues emerging from the study

(Continued)

> *(Continued)*
>
> Coordination was resource intensive. The practitioner researcher found that this took a great deal of time and the high level of diversity between different public service representatives led to extended exchanges to clarify issues. The practitioner researcher identified that the most useful task at the start of each phase of the study was to attempt to identify common ground. Once established the project could progress with a single purpose. Joined up thinking involving many agencies is not always straightforward and needs a single person with vision to hold all the pieces together.

Working collaboratively adds value to research; it strengthens research designs and promotes utilisation. Practitioner researchers should support the development of collaborative research projects after careful consideration to ensure that the research team is collegiate and all contributions are valued equally.

10.3 MARKETING RESEARCH

In Chapter 3 we discussed the factors that promote the initiation of successful change. These factors were identified as the need for change, clarity, complexity and practicality. This section builds upon these factors and discusses how practitioner researchers can lead change based on research. In order for research to be utilised it must be sold and practitioner researchers need to develop a strategy to market the research and findings. This should be done at the outset and take account of Weiss's (1986) models of research utilisation described in Box 10.1. To 'sell' research to practitioners and managers it must be packaged into a product. The product must then be made available to potential customers at a reasonable economic and psychological 'price'. The case study demonstrates the importance of thinking about marketing research.

> **Case Study:**
> **Nico – selling research**
>
> Nico is a practising health care professional. He qualified as a registered general nurse about six years ago. Currently, he is undertaking a Masters degree at a local university, within which he is required to undertake research related to his practice. Nico works in an emergency assessment unit in a district hospital. The unit receives patients in extremes of physiological crisis. In this
>
> *(Continued)*

(Continued)

setting Nico and his colleagues are required to deal with sudden and unpredictable critical situations, this includes people in heart failure requiring cardio-pulmonary resuscitation.

The frequent and spontaneous occurrence of crisis situations means that Nico and his colleagues have no opportunity for systematic debriefing after critical events. Staff rely on receiving limited, spontaneous support from colleagues and adopt individual strategies for attaining personal support.

Nico is conscious of the level of stress he experiences daily and has a growing concern about the effect of this stress on staff morale, sickness and performance for his colleagues. Nico researches stress within the workplace and prepares a report for his university course. He sends the report to the Trust management team who gratefully acknowledge the report and file it.

Disseminating research in an academic style is unlikely to be effective in a practice setting. Researchers who have spent long periods writing research reports may be disheartened when colleagues or managers fail to be enthused by the finer methodological issues encompassed within the study. The report that Nico prepares for the university offers a detailed account of the study, but is not necessarily appropriate to the Trust management team who are more likely to be concerned with implications of the findings. In order for Nico to market his research he needs first to create a product that can be 'sold'. A marketable product for his Trust might be: 'A strategy for improving support and supervision networks in the workplace.' This would be attractive to:

- Staff: colleagues would be interested in finding out how Nico's recommendations would improve the support they receive in the workplace
- Managers: the findings would provide managers with a strategy for reducing stress-related sickness and absenteeism and would improve recruitment and retention
- Organisation: Nico's study is timely in that attention in the NHS is focused on 'work–life balance' and looking after the psychological needs of staff. It is therefore politically appropriate, and the findings would be more likely to be perceived as useful (see 'the political model' in Box 10.1)

With the support of the Trust, Nico disseminates the product internally by writing a short article for the in-house staff journal. He also makes a series of short presentations to staff groups about the recommendations. Rather than making an academic presentation of the research and its findings, Nico designs a presentation where participants explore the recommendations in the context of their own workplace. Participants are encouraged to generate a list of benefits for themselves that would ensue from implementing the recommendations.

Nico's manager is aware that additional support and supervision as identified by the research would be costly and may have little impact in the short term. Nico agrees to produce a simple cost analysis and make a joint presentation, with his manager, to the management team to seek funding to develop and run a pilot study for support and supervision. Nico argues that not improving the support systems will lead to continued staff stress, high sickness and the poor management of risk. Improving the system as outlined in the recommendations would create a staff group who felt more supported and were able to work more effectively.

Different audiences, as was discussed in Chapter 9, perceive research differently. If practitioner researchers want to ensure that their research is utilised, then consideration must be given to how the research can be turned into a product to be sold to managers, colleagues, service users and any other stakeholders. This will not happen by chance, and the time practitioner researchers invest into selling the product will be recouped in the satisfaction and *kudos* of effective dissemination and utilisation.

10.4 MOTIVATION TO CHANGE

Change will not occur in the organisation unless the conditions present produce an adequate source of motivation. One such source may be the practitioner researcher. However, the practitioner researcher may not see the purpose of the research, its utilisation, as change. Instead it may be to reinforce or confirm the status quo. In addition, the motivation to adopt a change may not be the same for the practitioner researcher as for those within the change environment. Box 10.3 indicates the different sources of motivation.

Box 10.3   Conditions that may impact upon motivation to change

For the practitioner researcher

- The practitioner researcher has completed a funded project or completed a course and presented the results as a dissertation or research report. Undertaking the 'research' is the end itself

- Research utilisation is a 'performance task' required by senior managers

For the organization

- There is perceived value in maintaining the status quo/in the change

- The new change is perceived as relative to the volume and scope of other past, current or future change

- Competing forces, of differing strengths, within the environment are for/against the change

(Continued)

(Continued)

For the practitioner researcher

- Research utilisation is driven by the 'vision' of the practitioner researcher to bring about an improved service

For the organization

- Preparation for the change has/has not been undertaken
- There are pressures within the organisation to adopt the change. These pressures may be opposed and sabotaged or supported

As Box 10.3 indicates the practitioner researcher may be motivated by a number of factors. Practitioner researchers may find that, whilst trying to promote research utilisation in practice, their enthusiasm to carry through the particular change becomes depleted. They may need to examine their own motivation with regard to the research to ensure that there is adequate will to encourage utilisation.

Once practitioner researchers are aware of their own motivation for facilitating research utilisation the motivation that exists within practice should also be considered. If practitioner researchers are not familiar with these forces within practice, the chances of the change being successfully brought about are reduced. Awareness will enable them to better prepare others to accept changes to practice as a result of research findings.

Case Study 5:
Diane – managing competing forces

Diane has just completed research that demonstrates that newly qualified teachers (NQTs) value regular, structured meetings with a nominated mentor. The mentor is an experienced teacher who provides a safe and supportive environment in which new teachers can be self-critical in relation to their own teaching and develop new ways of addressing practice problems.

On completion of her research Diane has decided that the school in which she works would benefit from adopting the findings and recommendations of her work. She presents the work separately to the school governors, the service management team and her colleagues at a staff meeting. Everyone agrees that it is an interesting study and has major implications for the way in which NQTs begin their teaching careers. There is also general agreement that the work should be shared with a larger audience and Diane is encouraged to publish her work. Diane is, therefore, upset and confounded by the complete lack of enthusiasm or ability of everyone within the school to adopt her findings in practice.

If Diane had constructed a force field analysis she might have realised why there was a lack of enthusiasm for the work. Box 10.4 uses a 'force field analysis' (Lewin, 1951) to demonstrate how an environment unprepared for change will reject the change or, at least, render any change ineffective. Force field analyses assume that organisations come into stable state at a point where opposing forces are equal. The forces acting on stable state are power-based and derive from political, economic, social and technology domains. Change occurs when the forces for change exceed those for stability. Understanding how to mobilise forces to promote change is a valuable asset for practitioner researchers attempting to promote research utilisation.

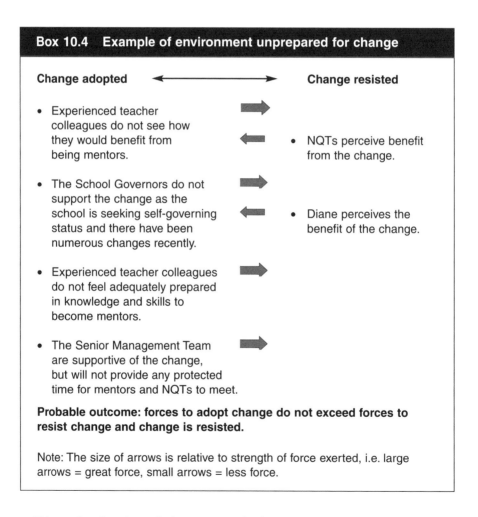

Box 10.4   Example of environment unprepared for change

Change adopted ←——————————→ **Change resisted**

- Experienced teacher colleagues do not see how they would benefit from being mentors.

    - NQTs perceive benefit from the change.

- The School Governors do not support the change as the school is seeking self-governing status and there have been numerous changes recently.

    - Diane perceives the benefit of the change.

- Experienced teacher colleagues do not feel adequately prepared in knowledge and skills to become mentors.

- The Senior Management Team are supportive of the change, but will not provide any protected time for mentors and NQTs to meet.

Probable outcome: forces to adopt change do not exceed forces to resist change and change is resisted.

Note: The size of arrows is relative to strength of force exerted, i.e. large arrows = great force, small arrows = less force.

Diane decides that, if change is to be brought about as a result of her research, she will have to put more effort into preparing the field and supporting the change. An examination of the force field suggests that there is nothing that can be done about the current pace of change; this is outside of Diane's control. The other factors can be explored further.

Diane returns to the Senior Management Team (SMT) and provides a more focused presentation with an approximate budget. She explains the significance of her findings in relation to current education targets and as innovative good practice. Following protracted negotiation the SMT agrees to undertake, and provide limited support for, the implementation of the findings in the form of a managed project, which Diane will oversee and evaluate.

Diane prepares a short information pack about the project that includes some information aimed at potential mentors. The information includes the preparatory training that mentors will receive and the on-going support that will be provided by a local higher education institution interested in supporting Diane to develop the project.

Diane meets with her experienced teacher colleagues. She presents the findings focusing on the benefits to her colleagues of working and learning with new staff. She explains the formation of the project and seeks a pool of volunteers who might be suitable to be part of the project and have access to the protected time offered by the SMT.

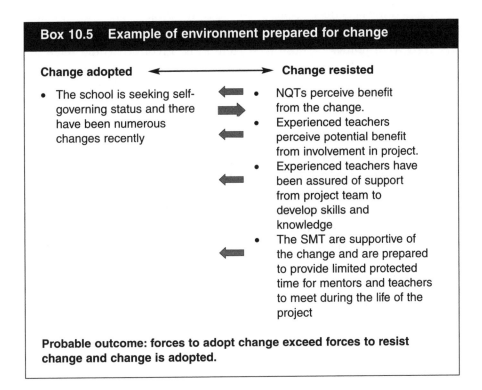

Box 10.5 Example of environment prepared for change

Change adopted ⟵⟶ **Change resisted**

- The school is seeking self-governing status and there have been numerous changes recently

- NQTs perceive benefit from the change.
- Experienced teachers perceive potential benefit from involvement in project.
- Experienced teachers have been assured of support from project team to develop skills and knowledge
- The SMT are supportive of the change and are prepared to provide limited protected time for mentors and teachers to meet during the life of the project

Probable outcome: forces to adopt change exceed forces to resist change and change is adopted.

Box 10.5 indicates how Diane has transformed the forces impacting upon her project and managed to create a situation where change is likely to be adopted. The construction of a force field analysis enables the competing forces to be examined in relation to one another. The model is simplistic and many forces may comprise both supportive and opposing forces. However, it enables practitioner researchers to focus their attention and energy on those parts of the organisation that need to shift their perception if the change is to occur.

10.5 CHANGE AND LEARNING ORGANISATIONS

There are a number of ways in which practitioner researchers may seek to implement change within their organisations. A typical approach might be to adopt the model described by Chin and Benne (1984) that incorporates: empirical–rational, normative–re-educative and power–coercive strategies.

The empirical–rational strategy regards people as rational beings who will adopt change when the benefits and incentives for doing so are perceived as advantageous and effectively communicated. Practitioner researchers using this strategy to encourage change emphasise the benefits of the change to those on whom the change will impact. In the earlier case study Diane emphasised the benefits of being involved in the project. The way in which she 'sold' the project was to make it apparent that those who were not involved were unlucky. Those who were to be involved would have the *kudos* of being in the project team, would have protected time to engage in mentoring and be able to shape the development of the project.

The normative–re-educative strategy assumes people will seek to follow whatever feels culturally appropriate; they will 'go with the flow'. This strategy requires practitioner researchers to bring about cultural change within the practice area; in effect, to create a situation where those who do not adopt the change feel 'left out', going 'against the flow'. Diane did not adopt this approach because cultural change is not a short-term strategy. Mentoring did not already exist within the school and Diane could, therefore, not demonstrate mentoring to be the cultural norm. She could have indicated examples from outside of the school where mentoring was culturally congruent. However, this would be limited in effectiveness as the dominant culture within the school, where the staff were employed, was not to mentor new staff. It would, therefore, be easier for staff to maintain allegiance to the dominant, non-mentoring, culture.

The power–coercive strategy seeks to control people through power and assumes people will generally do as they are told, particularly if punishment would be the result of failing to do as instructed. This is not a position that sits naturally with practitioner researchers, though the 'practitioner' part of the role may involve operational and strategic management. This change strategy is not available to Diane since she did not have the support of the school governors. In order to use this strategy Diane would require significant delegated powers to coerce people into adopting mentoring arrangements. This approach would probably have a negative impact on the nascent supervisory relationship required for effective mentoring.

The three strategies described by Chin and Benne (1984) can be applied with ease to work on individual research utilisation. Practitioner researchers may also be seeking to develop, within their areas of practice, a culture that is more flexible and accepting of change. Such a culture would be less concerned with individual projects as a continuous process of change and development. The learning organisation, as described by Senge (1990), achieves a continuous cycle of learning and change. This form of organisation engages in an ongoing process of innovation in practice. Senge's description of a learning organisation has not, to date, been supported by evidence of effectiveness (Iles and Sutherland, 2001). It remains, however, a popular aspiration for many public services.

Senge's work is underpinned by 'systems thinking', which fuses the elements of a learning organisation into a coherent body of theory and practice (Senge, 1990). For the practitioner researcher the use of systems thinking may be a valuable asset. Senge argues that an invisible fabric of interrelated actions binds human endeavour. Practitioner researchers may experience this interrelatedness when promoting research utilisation. Encouraging a team to integrate research findings into their practice will have a lasting impact on the development of practice, and the reverberations of that impact cannot be charted. Thus, research utilisation should not be undertaken without consideration of the potential future impact. Practitioner researchers must accept the same level of responsibility for research utilisation as they do for originating new research.

Bringing together the elements of a learning organisation will encourage practitioner researchers to construct and share visions of future practice with teams. By outlining the significance of the utilisation of specific research findings to others, the practitioner researcher will ensure that research utilisation does not occur through a one-off empirical rational strategy. It occurs, rather, as a shared and on-going endeavour toward a vision of improved practice.

SUMMARY

- Research utilisation is complex and there are many factors that will impact upon the utilisation of research findings
- Research does not become utilised without effort and strategic thinking

- Collaborative working with other professionals is an effective method of strengthening research designs. However, if practitioner researchers are not assertive, it may also result in practitioner researchers losing their voice in the design, delivery and utilisation of research
- Collaborative working promotes joined up thinking in addressing 'bigger issues'
- Developing a marketing strategy early on in practitioner research will facilitate the utilisation of research findings
- An understanding of the environment in which research is to be integrated is essential to effective utilisation
- Practitioner researchers should consider change as occurring within an interrelated system; change should therefore be brought about with consideration of the longer-term effects on the team

FURTHER READING

Iles, V. and Sutherland, K. (2001) *Organisational Change*. **London: NCCSDO**

Iles and Sutherland have produced a critical review of a number of different strategies for managing organisational change. The work provides a working overview of different strategies and identifies evidence in support of each model.

Katz, J. and Martin, B. (1997) 'What is research collaboration?', *Research Policy,* **26: 1–18**

Katz and Martin's paper provides an overview of how research collaboration can be achieved based on current practice.

11
Developing the Practitioner Researcher

This chapter addresses the issues of developing as a practitioner researcher. It takes as its starting point Kolb's (1984) 'learning cycle'. Adapting this for the practitioner researcher means that each of the stages can be used to ensure development. In particular the integration of reflection into each stage is important. The importance of reflection leading to reflexivity is explored. Finally, the use of supervision to aid development is reinforced.

The chapter focuses on:

- ⇨ How practitioners develop
- ⇨ Kolb's learning cycle
- ⇨ Reflection
- ⇨ Reflexivity
- ⇨ Techniques for developing reflective skills
- ⇨ Supervision

11.1 HOW PRACTITIONERS DEVELOP

Knowles (1970) identified the distinguishing features of how practitioners learn. Practitioners:

- Accumulate a growing reservoir of experience that becomes an increasing resource for learning
- Learning becomes increasingly oriented towards the actual role

- Self-concept changes from depending on others for learning to being self-directing
- Time perspective changes from one of postponed application to immediacy of application

These affect the way that practitioners develop research skills. Practitioners' actual experience of undertaking research becomes the central resource for developing further research skills. It is the experience of undertaking research that is central to the learning. Practitioners will be interested in developing research skills only if this is integrated into their work. Undertaking research for a higher degree is not likely in itself to help practitioners' readiness to learn. Practitioners also want to take ownership of their own learning rather than being dependent on others. Finally, practitioners will learn research skills best when they can immediately put them into practice. Practitioners need to see the immediate relevance of what is being learned.

Learning research skills therefore is not about simply reading a 'how-to' research book. It is a process not a single event. Kolb (1984) proposed a cyclical process for development with four core elements that are essential to the development (see Figure 11.1). This framework can be applied to the development of research skills. This starts with the development of a conceptual (or academic) problem-solving research framework and then through an understanding of the real world to the actual experience of undertaking research. The last link in the cycle is reflection on this experience, leading to refining and developing of the initial problem-solving research framework.

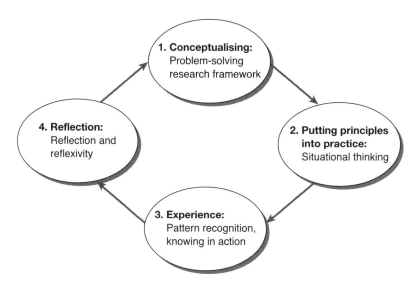

FIGURE 11.1 *Kolb's learning cycle*

11.2 KOLB'S LEARNING CYCLE

Step 1: Conceptualising

Practitioners require a way of conceptualising research and need to develop a problem-solving framework for research design. Most academic research courses provide such a framework as do many research textbooks. We have drawn upon a number of these, in particular Robson (2002) and Creswell (2003) to develop our own framework (see Chapter 7). The framework developed in Chapter 7 gives practitioner researchers a means of conceptualising the way their research can be undertaken.

Step 2: Putting Principles into Practice

The conceptualising process leads to general principles about how to undertake the research. However, these principles have to be modified according to the practice environment as there are always factors that affect the best way of carrying out research in any particular situation. Practitioners need to use their experience in order to be able to read particular situations in an organisation. In particular there are issues of the shadow side, as discussed in Chapter 4. In light of this, the research design may be modified and adapted in order to undertake effective research.

The argument for situational thinking has been put forcibly by Schon (1983, 1987). Professionals work in indeterminate zones of practice. Every situation is different and in any situation there are alternative ways of seeing things. Underpinning these different ways of seeing are alternative values. Schon argues that practitioners need artistry as well as rationality as the basis from which to work. This argument equally applies to practitioner research. The practitioner researcher needs a rational–technical framework for deciding on the purpose for their research and how it should be designed – this is the conceptualisation phase. However, the research is actually being undertaken in an indeterminate zone of practice in the shadow side and depends on the culture of the organisation and the stakeholders. The practitioner researcher needs to use artistry as well as rationality to ensure that the research is of value.

Schon's argument is that practitioners cannot learn how to act in any particular situation from formal teaching or a text book. This is because each situation is unique and practitioner researchers bring to each event their own particular way of working. Practitioner researchers learn by experience and reflection on the problems that they encounter both as practitioners and as researchers. The practitioner researcher needs to be able to put principles into practice by connecting up a theoretical framework with a particular practice context and their own relationship to the research.

Step 3: Experience

Dutton (1995) has developed a helpful model to understand how practitioners use their experience to develop their professional skills. This model highlights some of the difficulties that there are in using research experiences in the same way. She suggests that experienced professionals use a number of strategies to guide their practice when working with clients:

- Pattern recognition
- Knowing-in-action

Pattern recognition   Experienced practitioners analyse a problem to the point where they recognise familiar patterns. They mentally compare the story about the present problem to past problems. These stories take time to accumulate. Inexperienced practitioners need a supervisor, to give them stories, or need to use common sense and reflection to think about problems (see also Benner et al., 1999).

The major difference between this and developing research skills is the time frames the practitioner and researcher are working with. Practitioners, be they nurses, teachers or social workers, are likely to see the same type of problem on a very frequent basis – for example a pupil with behaviour problems or an adult who uses drugs. A repertoire of stories of how to address the problem may emerge fairly rapidly. A researcher, on the other hand, is likely to be working on far fewer research projects over the same number of years and therefore cannot easily accumulate the stories on 'how to do research'.

This means that most practitioner researchers' experiences of research come second-hand from reading research papers, from conferences or research presentations. The difficulty with this is that research papers or presentations rarely focus on the research process. Published papers usually gloss over the real difficulties that there were when undertaking the research apart from a sanitised version so often found under the heading 'Limitations of the Research'. The experience gained from reading or hearing presentations is not the same as the experience from doing.

Knowing-in-action   Dutton (1995) suggests that after an experienced practitioner has used pattern recognition to define the problem, the focus shifts to resolving the difficulty. Schon (1987) refers to the conventional routine through which the problem is addressed as knowing-in-action. Knowing-in-action is the knowledge that is revealed through actions. Knowing-in-action is how experienced practitioners practise throughout the day. It is used spontaneously without having to think through the problem from first principles (in other words it is like riding a bicycle). Schon makes the distinction between knowing-in-action (or reflection-in-action) and what he terms reflection-on-action. Reflection-on-action consists of thinking back on what one has done after the event.

For practitioner researchers engaged in research there is, however, a different process known as action-on-reflection. Action-on-reflection highlights that in research a good deal of time goes on reflection (thinking about what one is about to do) before action (undertaking the research). This is the reverse of the practitioner, where action has to be immediate, for example in a busy classroom or hospital ward, and reflection comes after. The discipline of undertaking a good deal of reflection, for example in the form of a plan or research proposal, can be difficult for the busy practitioner. Practitioners often wish to get on and actually undertake research before they have planned it out. As discussed in Chapter 7, this does not work. There is a need for practitioner researchers to ensure that the sequence is reflection (planning the research strategy) before action (undertaking the research), not the other way around.

It is helpful therefore to recognise that reflection is not simply at one point in this learning cycle but is interlinked throughout the process.

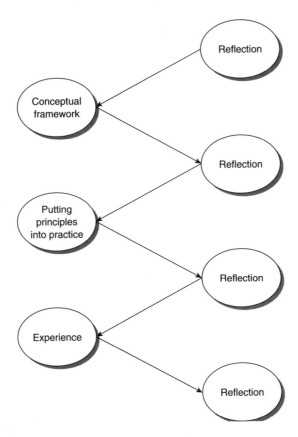

FIGURE 11.2   *Action on reflection in the learning cycle*

11.3 REFLECTION

'Reflection' has for a long time been a central concept in understanding how people develop (Boud et al., 1985). It has a number of meanings, but essentially reflection is a way in which people explore and clarify their experience in order to lead to a new understanding:

> Thinking about an experience with the intention of deciding what it means, how it can be explained and what the meaning and explanations might imply for the future. (Haigh, 1998)

Reflection should be used throughout the process of development as a practitioner researcher. Reflection can be done quite freely and informally. However, an initial structure helps to ensure that the important elements of the research experience are understood (see Box 11.1).

Box 11.1   Six cue questions for structured reflection

1. **What research have I undertaken?**
   Clarify what you have actually done.

2. **Why did I act the way I did?**
   Clarify why you behaved in the way you did at critical moments.
   Clarify if there is a distinction between why you behaved this way and the theoretical best way of undertaking the research.

3. **What are my feelings about the experience?**
   Clarify how the research is making you feel. Are you finding it a struggle, or disappointing or unsatisfying?
   Having ascertained the feelings you can begin to think about where they are coming from.

4. **What have you learnt from this experience?**
   Clarify what has been learned.
   How has your conceptual framework changed?
   How has your reading of this particular situation changed?

5. **What sense do you make of this experience?**
   Clarify the meaning for you as a practitioner researcher of this research.
   How has this research experience changed who you are?

6. **What is my plan?**
   How does this last research experience affect my plan for this research?
   What do I need to do now to help me with this research and with future research?

Reflection may appear at first sight to be a passive process. However, it is a process that should lead to action. Through reflection the practitioner researcher thinks through a past experience in order to plan how to deal with similar experiences in the future.

Case Study:
Mario's reflections on running a focus group

Mario works for a Children Service and has been researching parents' views about bringing up children. He has finished his research report but takes time to reflect on his research by using the six cue questions.

1. **What research have I undertaken?**
   I was running a focus group with both male and female members. I wanted to hear about their experiences of bringing up children within an inner city. However, after a while the men became silent. They lost their voice.

2. **Why did I act the way I did?**
   There are two aspects to this. Why I set up focus groups and how I acted when I was actually running the groups. There were some women-only focus groups but this one was deliberately mixed to hear the men's voices. When I was in the group I did not stop and feed back my concerns to the group. Instead I tried to make eye contact with the men to encourage them to talk.

3. **What are my feelings about this experience?**
   I am embarrassed at losing the potential voice of the men. I identified with them and wanted them to have a voice.

4. **What have I learned from this experience?**
   I should have insisted with the research commissioners that we had a male-only group. I could also have structured the focus group differently and ensured that everyone had a voice.

5. **What sense do I make of this experience?**
   I lost the meaning of this experience by being annoyed that the men did not speak. In retrospect the men not speaking was the most important thing that came out of the research. Men could not speak about childrearing in front of women.

6. **What is my plan?**
   I need to go back and listen to the audio tapes again. I must try to make sense of the men's silence and incorporate that into the research report. In future I must remember that what is not said may be as helpful in research terms as what is said. I must reflect on my sense of the audio tapes once I have listened to them again!

In some types of research reflection is central to the process of undertaking the research. In particular both action research and many types of qualitative research use reflection as an active part of the process.

11.4   REFLEXIVITY

It is important to distinguish between reflection and reflexivity. Reflection is the process of monitoring or thinking about research as a way of understanding and changing future research practice.

Reflexivity, on the other hand, is about understanding how research is affected, in terms of outcomes and process, by one's own position as a researcher. Reflexivity refers to the observer/observed dynamic. Reflexivity proposes that one's identity and lived reality reflect one another, that is, that they are co-constructed. In other words the beliefs of researchers affect the world that they research. Conversely, the world that they research affects their thoughts and beliefs. The two are interdependent – the observer and the observed.

Reflexivity is of central importance in interpretative qualitative research:

> [T]he researcher filters the data through a personal lens that is situated in a specific sociopolitical and historical moment. One cannot escape the personal interpretations brought to qualitative data analysis. (Creswell, 2003: 182)

In order to understand the data the qualitative researcher needs to be introspective through a process of reflection on his or her own personal place in the research.

Types of Reflexivity

Depending upon the research perspective there are different types of reflexivity (see Finlay, 2002 for a fuller description). From a phenomenological perspective reflexivity is about understanding oneself and one's impact on the research experience. On the other hand, in social constructional research reflexivity is used to understand the researcher's relationship to the research design and theory and how it is co-constructed. It is also used in social constructional research to understand the researcher's relationship to the research participants and how the data and the analysis of it were consciously and unconsciously co-constructed (see Figure 11.3).

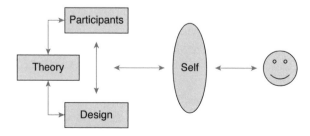

FIGURE 11.3   *Types of reflexivity*

The phenomenological perspective Phenomenologists are interested in the subjectivity of experiences. Put a number of researchers in the same situation and each will experience and understand it differently. Each researcher will bring to a research experience specific subjective meanings depending on their past experiences. Some of these reactions will be conscious and some unconscious. From a phenomenological perspective, practitioner researchers need first to understand themselves if they are to understand their own research. The goal is not the elimination of subjectivity but the understanding of it in order to understand how it has affected the research.

Case Study:
Phenomenological reflexivity in teenage suicide

Sanghita, a practitioner researcher, undertakes a piece of exploratory research on teenagers who attempt suicide. It is designed around flexible, open-ended interviews with teenagers who have attempted suicide. There are certain set areas for the interviews but the research is designed to explore the material that the teenagers bring up. The research is specifically designed to allow Sanghita to ask different questions and follow up on responses by the interviewees.

On reflection Sanghita realises that some interviews took much longer than others. She also realises that there were certain teenagers whose experiences she was more interested in. She then begins to realise that there are certain aspects of attempted suicide that she is fascinated by and on further reflection realises that she herself had similar passing thoughts as a teenager, particularly throwing herself onto railway lines.

Further reflection helps Sanghita to recognise that she had not built on previous published research in this area as this aspect of teenage suicide was not usually dealt with. Open-ended interviews had been chosen because it would allow her to explore this powerful but long neglected area of interest for her.

The social constructionist perspective Social constructionists are interested in how the research has been co-constructed. This co-construction occurs at a number of levels. Fundamentally it occurs between the practitioner researcher and the stakeholders, particularly the participants. In addition the research design is co-constructed between the practitioner researcher and previous researchers. The researcher, through his or her reading of previous research, tries to produce a valid research design. This though is not done through intuition or inspiration but through co-construction. The practitioner researcher needs to understand how and why he or she co-constructed the research the way they did. This is known as the reflexive nature of the research.

Examples of co-construction come from participatory approaches as discussed in Chapter 3. These paradigms explicitly involve participants as co-researchers. Some of the paradigms, for example co-operative enquiry (Heron, 1996), explicitly use a cycle of enquiry that includes reflection to induce reflexivity. Researchers and participants need to understand how their different positions will affect what they see and make sense of. Participatory enquiry explicitly acknowledges that the difference between the researcher and the participant in terms of race, gender, class and power will affect their research.

Being Reflexive throughout the Research

Practitioner researchers need to be reflective throughout the research to demonstrate their reflexivity. It is not something simply to think about at the end.

To become more reflexive, reflect on the following questions about a piece of research that you are involved in.

    ☐ **Pre-research stage**
         Why is this research area important for you?
         What are your assumptions about what you will find?
         What theories do you have to make sense of this area?
         What do you not want to find out/hear?

    ☐ **Research design and data collection**
         Why did you choose this particular design?
         What did you hope to get from it?
         In an ideal world how would this design have been different?

    ☐ **Data analysis**
         How did the relationship with the participants affect the data collection?
         How did these interviews make you feel?
         Which interviews were different?
         At what points did you change your thinking on the issue?

    ☐ **Writing up**
         Who are you writing this for?
         Who do you hope will *not* read it?
         What sort of film would this make?
         To whom is it dedicated (metaphorically)?

The Dangers of Reflexivity

Reflexivity is a complex process. The danger is that one starts to reflect on oneself, then on oneself on the research, then on the self that is a reflection on the self on the research, and so on *ad infinitum*. Practitioner researchers can end up being more preoccupied by their own thoughts and emotional reactions than they are by the research participants and their data (Finlay, 2002). Reflexivity is crucial to practitioner researchers understanding their own place in their own research. It is a process, however, to achieve clarity not to create confusion or self-centred introspection.

Reflexivity is about being aware of one's own reasons for constructing knowledge in particular ways. It is about being aware of one's own values and motivations, and the social, cultural and political context in which one makes decisions about what is valid about the research and the way the research was carried out.

11.5 TECHNIQUES FOR DEVELOPING REFLECTIVE SKILLS

Reflection has two main interrelated purposes. One of these is related to the process of undertaking the research. The other is to do with the practitioner researcher's development as a researcher. The previous sections highlighted that, depending upon the type of research, there are three levels of reflection:

- Reflection on research experience
- Reflection on self – phenomenological reflexivity
- Reflection on self in research experience – socially constructed reflexivity

There are a number of techniques that can aid reflection. Many of these are helped by keeping a research diary (see Chapter 9).

Box 11.3   Techniques for aiding reflection and reflexivity

- Developing a systemic perspective through rich pictures
- Seeing the patterns in research through diary analysis
- Understanding the root cause through a Why/Why diagram
- Making sense of the research through asking circular questions

---

Developing a systemic perspective through rich pictures

The research and the practitioner researcher are part of multiple systems. Chapter 4 showed how there needs to be an understanding of the interconnectedness of the research to these other systems. Rich pictures are able to capture the essence of complex, messy situations and are very good at describing the experiences of research. They can capture in an easy visual way the essence of what the practitioner researcher did and how people reacted to the research.

Technique: rich pictures
Draw a rich picture

☑ Where are you in the research?
☑ How have people reacted to the research?
☑ What barriers are there in the way of you completing it?

Seeing the patterns in research through diary analysis

There are patterns in life. Organisations, as well as people, often repeat ways of behaving. So some organisations repetitively reconfigure themselves, and people become involved in the same destructive arguments at work (as well as home). The practitioner researcher will also repeat patterns of behaviour in research. One of the ways of understanding research is to see these patterns. These patterns may be to do with how time is managed, mood swings from excitement to despair, or stakeholders' reactions to the research.

Technique: Diary analysis
Keep a research diary:

☑ What patterns keep reoccurring?
☑ Are there events, or feelings, thoughts or doubts?
☑ What holds the patterns together?

Understanding the root cause through a Why/Why diagram

Any problem with research is only a problem because it is given meaning as a problem. Difficulties such as recruiting participants, or making sense of data, are almost certainly underpinned by more fundamental issues.

Technique: Why/Why

Start with any issue or problem:

☐ Ask 'Why is this a problem?' Then ask 'Why' again and then again. As the question 'Why' is asked, the nature of the problem changes. This will gradually uncover the really big issues that give it meaning.

Making sense of the research through asking circular questions

Questions need to be asked about the research. Some of these questions will be descriptive, for example, 'How did the manager react to my suggestion for focus groups?'. In systemic literature this is a type of circular question. Circular questions explore the connections between an individual and the organisation. In practitioner research they can be used to explore the relationship between the research, the participants, the organisation and the researcher.

Technique: circular questions

☐ **Hypothesising**: What is going on in this research?
I have a hunch that the issue with this research …
And therefore I am interested in finding out more …

☐ **Reframing**: How can I see this research differently?
If I asked … [supervisor, participant, manager] about this research experience they would say …

☐ **Future questions**: Where will this research be in the future?
Six months from now where will I be with this research?

The above techniques are all useful to aid reflection on research. However, practitioners have a range of other techniques that they use to understand the people they work with and these can also be used to make sense of the research.

11.6 SUPERVISION

Types of Supervision

Most practitioners receive supervision for their professional practice. The issue is how supervision can also be used to help develop practitioner researchers' research skills.

> It [supervision] can give us a chance to stand back and reflect; a chance to avoid the easy way out of blaming others – clients, peers, the organisation, 'society', or even oneself; and it can give us a chance to engage in the search for new options, to discover the learning that often emerges from the most difficult situations and to get support. (Hawkins and Shohet, 2000: 3)

Hawkins and Shohet (2000) distinguish three different types of supervision:

* **Educative:** to develop the skills, understanding and abilities of the researcher
* **Supportive**: to ensure the researcher is not left to carry difficulties or problems alone
* **Managerial:** to ensure research standards are met; this includes ensuring quality and ethical standards are met and that time is used effectively

These three types should overlap for most research supervisors. Different aspects may, however, be emphasised depending upon the supervisor's role.

The Supervision Contract

Practitioner researchers should clarify the type of supervision they need through developing a supervision contract with the research supervisor. This contract does not need to be written but should be openly discussed. The contract addresses four areas.

* **Practicalities**: What are the frequency, length, place and time of each supervision session? What might postpone or interrupt a session?
* **Boundaries**: What will be talked about in the session? The research – of course – but what about practitioner or personal issues that may impact on the research?
* **The session format**: What will a particular session look like? Does the practitioner researcher bring areas of research experience that he or she wishes to reflect on? Does the practitioner researcher only bring the problems he or she has? Will data be looked at? How much, if any, of each session is about planning ahead? Will a record be kept of supervision and if so by whom?
* **The organisational and professional context**: What is your organisation's policy on research supervision? Does the organisation have expectations on what supervision should do? How do issues of confidentiality affect the supervision? This may be particularly an issue in academic institutions or in the NHS under research governance rules.

Though agreeing a supervision contract may seem unnecessary and rather bureaucratic, it is very helpful and we recommend it as good practice. The process of discussing these four areas helps avoid misunderstandings. For example, if the supervisor is part of an academic institution then the researcher needs to know if a record is kept by the supervisor, especially if this record will be referred to when considering proceeding to the next stage of the course.

Complete the following sentences:

    ☐   My hope for supervision is …

    ☐   What I fear happening in supervision is …

Discuss these with your supervisor

A Process Model of Supervision

Hawkins and Shohet (2000) have developed a very elegant supervision model. This can be adapted and simplified for this work on supervising practitioner research. Essentially the model suggests that there are four factors in supervision (see Figure 11.4):

- A supervisor
- A practitioner researcher
- The research
- A work context

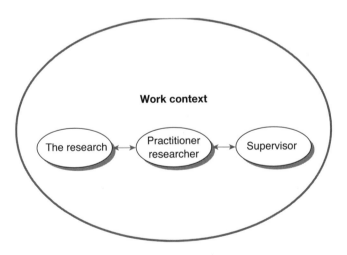

FIGURE 11.4   *Four factors in supervision*

Tasks for Supervision

The first task of supervision is to help to understand the connection between the practitioner researcher and the research. The supervision can focus on the first three questions from the six cue questions for structured reflection (see Box 11.1). Supervision should prompt reflection and act as another lens through which research can be seen.

The second task of supervision is to make a connection between the process of supervision and the process of research. This leads practitioner researchers to have greater understanding of themselves in terms of reflexivity. The focus is on understanding the relationship between the practitioner researcher and the supervisor and how that will reflect some of the issues in undertaking the research. To do this supervision can focus on two aspects of the process:

- The researcher's internal processes
- Supervision as a parallel to the research process

Focus on the researcher's internal processes   The focus here is on where the beliefs and feelings that the practitioner researchers have about their research are coming from. In particular, the concept of transference is helpful here. This notion is that people transfer previous emotional experiences of similar situations (which may be research situations) to how they feel and think about the present situation. A practitioner researcher may feel dejected because the statistical analysis that he or she is trying to do has an emotional underpinning of how hopeless they felt about maths in school. Or the interviews a practitioner researcher is conducting with people who have suffered heart attacks may become reminders of his or her own mortality. Central to this aspect of supervision is recognising that the practitioner researcher is unlikely to be aware of why he or she is feeling this way.

In the same way, beliefs about what is good (and bad) research may be locked in a particular way of seeing oneself. So, for example, it may be difficult to see oneself as an empathetic and empowering practitioner if one's research seems to be objective and disempowering for a particular vulnerable group. Understanding how beliefs about oneself and research are affecting one's experience of undertaking research is the sort of complex experience that good supervision can make sense of.

Focus on supervision as a parallel to the research process   The focus here is on how the process of supervision may reflect the way the researcher undertakes research. Researchers who come to supervision with a list of points to cover may also be seeing the research process in the same organised way. Vice versa, researchers who come to supervision disorganised and ill at ease may reflect how they are handling the research.

In addition to the above, supervisors should focus on their own internal processes. The supervisor may also have complex and mixed feelings about the research. How does the supervisor feel and deal with the practitioner researcher who chooses a methodology unfamiliar to the supervisor? For example, how does the supervisor feel when confronted with a particular sophisticated statistical method, an obscure type of qualitative data analysis, or action research? Does the supervisor have feelings of betrayal or competition with the supervisee? Does he or she feel anxious at the thought of a session with the practitioner researcher, or bored or excited? Where do those feelings come from? What do they tell the supervisor about the nature of the relationship with the practitioner researcher and the research? Are these feelings a reflection of how the researcher feels, that is, bored or excited also, or is the supervisor bringing in his or own boredom with supervising research? Supervisors are part of the supervision process. Practitioner researchers need to understand this and through their supervision contract ensure openness and transparency applies to their supervision as much as to their research.

Developing as a skilled practitioner researcher requires effort and thought. It can only happen in the context of undertaking research. To start the cyclical process of development the practitioner researcher needs the courage to break into the cycle and start the research.

SUMMARY

To develop, practitioner researchers need to:

- Ensure research is integrated into one's working role
- Recognise that development as a researcher is a process not an event
- Use Kolb's cyclical model as a framework for development
- Use reflection at each stage of development but particularly at the end
- Turn reflection into reflexivity
- Use a variety of innovative techniques to aid reflection
- Clarify the nature of research supervision in order to use supervision effectively to develop as a reflexive researcher

FURTHER READING

Hawkins, P. and Shohet, R. (2000) *Supervision in the Helping Professions.* **Buckingham: Open University Press**

This classic book on supervision does not specifically deal with research supervision. However, for the practitioner researcher it provides a wealth of information and ideas on how to ensure the best from supervision.

12
Conclusions

Practitioner Research and Development

Practitioner research provides a vehicle for practitioners to examine their practice and challenge the assumptions on which that practice is constructed. Such an approach is entirely consistent with professional practice and continuous professional development. Change and development are integral to both research and practice with practitioner researchers being present in the field and engaging with an extension of Kolb's experiential learning cycle, as described in Figure 12.1.

As evidence-based practice develops as an integral part of public service delivery, practitioner research is becoming increasingly significant within health, education and social care services. Practitioner researchers, as has been demonstrated, encounter many problems when engaging with the current research landscape in the public services, and many of these problems are new and without precedence. Within this book we have highlighted that structures currently in place to govern research have adversely impacted upon innovative research. We believe that practitioner research should and will grow into an increasingly significant aspect of personal and professional development within health, education and social care services. The development of this new research tradition will have wide implications in the development of public services.

Practitioners who have carried out research and researchers who happen also to be practitioners have always been present in public services. The practitioner researcher, however, is different. The practitioner researcher thinks about practice and research from a position that is different to academic researchers. The role is underpinned by reflexivity that comes from the proximity of the practitioner to the field of research. Practitioner

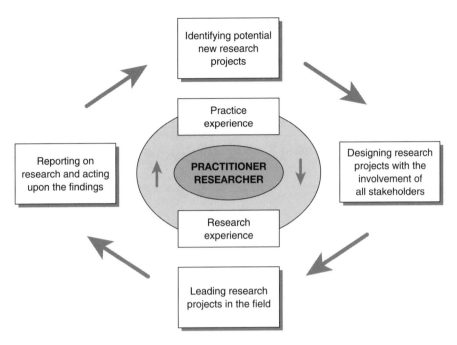

FIGURE 12.1 *Practitioner researcher's experiential learning and the research cycle*

researchers as employees within the public services undertake research that begins and ends with practice. This is what gives it its distinct character.

This book has highlighted some of the hazards associated with practitioner research. Practitioner researchers are surrounded by people who have vested interests in the research. In traditional research relationships the researcher engages with the field only during the research. For the practitioner, engagement occurs before, during and after research. The practitioner researcher has the benefit of a deep understanding of the field, but also has to work with the consequences of the research. We regard this as a strong point of practitioner research. Living with the consequences of research makes practitioner researchers more conscientious about values in relation to current research participants and the future impact of their work.

Support for and Collaboration with Practitioner Researchers

The greatest problem for practitioner researchers is overcoming the fear of 'being found out'. This is a common problem for many people, whether they are actors, politicians or professionals. Practitioners often feel uneasy that the limits to their research knowledge and experience will be exposed and that they will be shown up as incompetent, or at least unskilled, researchers. Becoming a practitioner researcher means recognising that fear and facing it.

Practitioner researchers can also find themselves very isolated. There are few practitioners who would claim to be 'expert' researchers so the enthused, but fledgling, practitioner researcher may lack a mentor who can offer knowledgeable support in the field. The relationship between academic researchers and practitioner researchers may be undermined by poor communication and lack of awareness of each other's worlds. We believe that the development of effective support networks is imperative to the growth of practitioner research.

Therefore there is a need for collaboration with higher education, the traditional bastion of research expertise. Increasingly, universities are recognising the commercial value of acknowledging and responding to this need. They are supporting and facilitating the growth of practitioner research and practitioner researchers and collaborating in the production of good quality, original research even when it does not correspond with the current hierarchy of knowledge promulgated within the health, education and social services.

The practitioner researcher also needs to establish collaborative relationships with the service users. Service users have a key role to play in practitioner research and research done without their involvement has major limitations when it is applied in practice. Without a genuine collaboration with the service user the practitioner researcher will not be able to use the research to drive change in practice that will be accepted by the service user. If collaboration with service users is to move beyond tokenism, it will entail ceding some control and ownership to service users. In this sense, practitioner research is quite different from the traditional research paradigm that views service users as research subjects. Whilst this is a major strength of practitioner research, it can be difficult to achieve. Establishing meaningful collaboration with service users is challenging but we would argue that it should be seen as an integral part of practitioner research.

In addition to service users, the practitioner researcher needs to engage with other stakeholders in order for research to bring about a change in practice. In the current climate of multidisciplinary teams and 'joined up working' between agencies there may be a large number of diverse stakeholders to engage with. 'Joined up research', where practitioners from different disciplines come together to research a common issue, can be a highly effective mechanism to promote multidisciplinary teams in practice. By developing a shared understanding of an issue through researching it together practitioners are likely to extend such shared understanding into working together.

Practitioner Research and Values

Underpinning any research there are subtle issues about determining what is of value. The issue of what is of value is not as straightforward as it might appear at first sight.

The problem of defining what is of value has been well illustrated by Robinson (1993). She takes an example from education to demonstrate that to attain a definition of 'improvement' is highly complex. The example she uses is 'The Reading Recovery Programme' developed in New Zealand and extensively used in New Zealand, Australia, the United States of America and in the UK. 'Reading Recovery' is an individualised reading and writing programme for children who have the lowest level of reading achievement after one year in school. Extensive research carried out by Marie Clay (1990) and others has consistently shown the benefits of the programme in terms of the improvement of reading levels of children who have taken part. This would seem to show conclusively that the programme is of value. However, whether the programme is useful or not depends, as Robinson (1993) points out, on what is considered of value. If the problem is the low reading skills of some children after a year of school and the solution the improvement of these skills then 'Reading Recovery' may be considered successful. If, on the other hand, the problem is seen as the inappropriate whole class teaching of reading to 5-year-olds, or the size of the class that infant teachers are expected to teach, then the 'Reading Recovery' programme does not become a solution, but rather a distraction from the real problems.

The key point for the practitioner researcher is that research is not a neutral activity. The way the practitioner researcher formulates the research questions directs research into particular areas.

Schon's (1987) description of the difficulties for professionals working in complex messy situations can be equally applied to practitioner researchers. Schon emphasised that different values will lead to different outcomes for different people. So, for some people, draining a swamp may be a solution, but for others this may be an ecological disaster. In our world, the elderly 'bed blocker' may also be someone who needs rehabilitation, or the excluded pupil may become the drug-selling teenager. In other words, what may seem a positive outcome for one particular service may for someone else create significant problems. This is why there is great importance in connecting one's own values as a researcher to those from other services (Lomax, 1994).

Changing Practice

Argyris and Schon (1974) described two levels of change, which can be helpfully equated with two different levels of research. The first is single-loop learning (connected to first-order research). Single-loop learning, or change, is what happens when the practitioner (or an organisation) makes adjustments in what they presently do. This often involves changing a target or standard to be met by the introduction of a new service or programme.

Measuring the success of our research by a rise in reading ages or a reduced length of stay in hospital is an example of first-order research. First-order research does not require a change of beliefs or values.

On the other hand, double-loop learning (connected to second-order research) occurs only when the practitioner examines their underpinning value system. Double-loop learning or change is very unlikely to occur unless the research methodology actually engages with the values of research espoused by the practitioner (Robinson, 1993). So practitioners may justify their position not to change by claiming that the research methodology was not valid, for example that the research did not use a randomised control led trial. In this way practitioners and others, such as managers and politicians, can justify never changing their practice if it goes against their values. However, if it is the practitioner who has designed and undertaken the research, as a practitioner researcher, the complex process of second order change is facilitated.

In order for double-loop learning to occur, practitioners need to be aware of the values that underpin their own and their profession's practice. Single-loop change can be imposed downwards (through, for example, policy directives) if the practitioners' values are not challenged. Double-loop change that requires people to shift their values will not occur unless practitioners validate the research methodology. Actively involving professionals in research through practitioner research helps ensure that second order change will occur.

Coming Out of the Shadows

In this book we have argued that practitioners in health, education and social care services should increasingly be in the forefront of developing the evidence base for their own professional practice. How they do this will depend on their view of what is good quality research and ultimately therefore on their views of knowledge.

Evidence-based practice is used here in its widest form rather than the 'randomised controlled trial' dominated agenda that currently pervades the health service. Practitioner research has the capacity to challenge the values that maintain the status quo of research within the public sector.

Schon's (1987) distinction between espoused theories and theories-in-use is particularly helpful here. It appears that professionals' espoused theory about practice is usually constructional. It starts from a premise that there are many different ways of seeing (constructing) the world and appropriate interventions are matched to the individual clients (patients, pupils or service users). This seems to work when the view of the client and the professional are in accord.

However, if the client constructs the problem differently, then the professional may flip to a positivist position. This can be seen as the theory-in-use, the theory which those around professionals see them using. The professionals defend their new position based on theoretical knowledge founded on policy based on positivist research evidence. So the health professional who thinks that a patient is ready to go home from hospital will state a constructional position that discharge from hospital should occur only when the patient is ready. But, depending on circumstances, for example bed availability or motivation of the patient to return home, the professional may flip to a positivist-based position.

Practitioners need to become more actively involved in creating their own evidence base. This requires three commitments:

- A commitment to researching individual practice as the starting point for a proper evidence-based profession
- A commitment to researching individual services in order to create an evidence base that is situated within context
- A commitment to establishing professional networks to amass a body of good quality research that will enable the current hegemony of research in the public services to be challenged

We do not propose that practitioner research replaces existing research in the public services, but that it takes its rightfully valued place alongside existing research. We would maintain that it is through practitioners researching their own practice, their own service and their own profession, that positive change will happen in the public services.

References

Argyris, C. and Schon, D. (1974) *Theory into Practice.* San Francisco: Jossey-Bass.

Barnes, J., Stein, A. and Rosenberg, W. (1999) 'Evidence based medicine and evaluation of mental health services: methodological issues and future directions', *Archives of Disease in Childhood*, 80: 280–5.

Benner, P., Hooper-Kyriakidis, P. and Stannard, D. (1999) *Clinical Wisdom and Interventions in Critical Care.* Philadelphia: W.B. Sanders.

Beresford, P. (2001) 'User involvement and social care research: Consumers in NHS Research News, Winchester', *Consumers in NHS Research* (NHS R&D).

Beresford, P. (2003) *It's Our Lives: A Short Theory of Knowledge, Distance and Experience.* London: Citizen Press in association with Shaping Our Lives.

Bhaskar, R. (1975) *A realist theory of science.* Brighton: Harvester.

Boud, D., Keogh, R. and Walker, D. (eds) (1985) 'Writing and reflection', in *Reflection: Turning Experience into Learning.* London: Kogan Page.

Bradbury, F. (1933) *Causal Factors in Tuberculosis.* London: National Association for the Prevention of Tuberculosis.

Bristol Royal Infirmary Inquiry (2001) *Learning from Bristol: the Report of the Public Inquiry into Children's Heart Surgery at the Bristol Royal Infirmary, 1984–1995.* Command Paper CM 5207. Published by the Bristol Royal Infirmary Inquiry.

Brydon-Miller, M. (2001) 'Education, research and action', in D. Tolman and M. Brydon-Miller (eds), *From Subjects to Subjectivities: A Handbook of Interpretive and Participatory Methods.* London: New York University Press.

Bury, M. (forthcoming) 'Chronic illness, expert patients and care transition', *Sociology of Health and Illness.*

Butler, J. (2003) 'Research in the place where you work – some ethical issues', *Bulletin of Medical Ethics,* 185: 21–2.

Campbell, D. and Stanley, J. (1963) 'Experimental and quasi-experimental designs for research', in N. Gage (ed.), *Handbook of Research on Teaching.* Chicago: Rand–McNally. pp. 1–76.

Carper, B. (1978) 'Fundamental patterns of knowing in nursing', *Advances in Nursing Science,* 1 (1): 13–23.

Carr, W. (1989) 'Action research: ten years on', *Journal of Curriculum Studies*, 21 (1): 85–90.

Chalmers, I. (1995) 'What do I want from health research and researchers when I am a patient?', *British Medical Journal,* 310: 1315–18.

Checkland, P. and Scholes, J. (1990) *Soft Systems Methodology in Action.* Chichester: Wiley.

Chin, R. and Benne, K. (1984) 'General strategies for effecting change in human systems', in W. Bennis, K. Benne and R. Chin (eds), *The Planning of Change*, 4th edition. New York: Holt, Rinehart & Winston.

Clark, A.M. (1998) 'The qualitative–quantitative debate: moving from positivism and confrontation to post-positivism and reconciliation', *Journal of Advanced Nursing*, 27 (6): 1242–9.

Clarke, A. (1999) *Evaluation Research: An Introduction to Principles, Methods and Practice*. London: Sage.

COREC (2006) 'Implementing the recommendations of the Ad Hoc Advisory Group'. Consultation. www.corec.org:uk/consultation/implementationplancansultation.pdf (accessed February 2006)

Corey, S. (1953) *Action Research to Improve School Practice*. New York: Teachers College, Columbia University.

Creswell, J. (2003) *Research Design: Qualitative, Quantitative and Mixed Methods Approaches*. London: Sage.

Dadds, M. (2006) 'Perspectives on Practitioner Research – Development and Enquiry Programmes – Teacher Researchers'. www.ncl.org.uk.ncl (accessed February 2006).

DfEE (1998) *Excellence in Research on Schools*. London: The Stationery Office.

Department of Health (2005a) *Report of the Ad Hoc Advisory Group on the Operation of NHS Research Ethics Committee*. London: Department of Health.

Department of Health/National Health Service (2005b) *Creating a Patient-led NHS – Delivering the NHS Improvement Plan*. London: Department of Health.

Department of Health (2006) *Best Research for Best Health – A New National Health Research Strategy*. London: Department of Health.

Deshler, D. and Grudens-Schuck, N. (2000) 'The politics of knowledge construction', in A. Wilson and E. Hayes (eds), *Handbook of Adult and Continuing Education*. San Francisco: Jossey–Bass.

Dick, B. and Swepson, P. (1994) 'Appropriate validity and its attainment within action research: an illustration using soft systems methodology', www.scu.edu.au/schools/gcm/ar/arp/sofsys2.html (accessed February 2006).

Dowie, J. and Elstein, A. (eds) (1998) *Professional Judgement*. Cambridge: Cambridge University Press.

Dutton, R. (1995) *Clinical Reasoning in Physical Disabilities*. London: Williams and Wilkins.

Egan, G. (1994) *Working the Shadow Side*. San Francisco: Jossey–Bass.

Elliott, J. (1978) 'What is action research in schools?', *Journal of Curriculum Studies*, 10 (4): 355–7.

Elliott, R., Fischer, C. and Rennie, D. (1999) 'Evolving guidelines for publication of qualitative research studies in psychology and related fields', *British Journal of Clinical Psychology*, 38: 215–29.

Eraut, M. (1994) *Developing Professional Knowledge and Competence*. London: Routledge–Falmer.

Evans, C., Mellor-Clark, J., Margison, F., Barkham, M., Audin, K., Connel, J. and McGrath, G. (2000) 'CORE: Clinical Outcomes in Routine Evaluation', *Journal of Mental Health*, 9 (3): 247–55.

Evans, G. (2001) 'A rationale for oral care', *Nursing Standard*, 15: 33–6.

Fine, M., Weis, L., Weseen, S. and Wong, L. (2000) 'For Whom? Qualitative research, representations and social responsibilities', in N. Denzin and Y. Lincoln (eds), *Handbook of Qualitative Research*. Thousand Oaks, CA: Sage. pp. 107–31.

Finlay, L. (2002) '"Outing" the researcher: the provenance, process, and practice of reflexivity', *Qualitative Health Research*, 12 (4): 531–45.

Fraser, D.M. (1997) 'Ethical dilemmas and practical problems for the practitioner researcher', *Educational Action Research*, 5 (1): 161–71.

Freshwater, D. and Rolfe, G. (2001) 'Critical reflexivity: a politically and ethically engaged research method for nursing', *NT Research*, 6 (1): 526–37.

Fullan, M. (2001) *The New Meaning of Educational Change*, 3rd edition. London: Cassell.

Furlong, J. and Oancea, A. (2005) *Assessing Quality in Applied and Practice Based Educational Research – a Framework for Discussion*. Oxford: Oxford University Department of Education.

Gabe, J., Bury, M. and Elston, M. (2004) *Key Concepts in Medical Sociology*. London: Sage.

Ghaye, T. and Lillyman, S. (2000a) *Caring Moments: The Discourse of Reflective Practice*. Dinton: Quay Books.

Ghaye, T. and Lillyman, S. (2000b) *Reflection: Principles and Practice for Healthcare Professionals*. Dinton: Quay Books.

Ghaye, T., Gillespie, D. and Lillyman, S. (2000) *Empowerment through Reflection*. Dinton: Quay Books.

Glaser, B. and Strauss, A. (1967) *The Discovery of Grounded Theory: Strategies for Qualitative Research*. Chicago: Aldine.

Glazer, N. (1974) 'The schools of the minor professions', *Minerva,* 12: 346–64.

Glen, S. and Wilkie, K. (eds) (2000) *Problem-based Learning in Nursing*. London: Macmillan.

Green, G. (1998) 'Bridging the gap during the interview process'. *Feminism & Psychology,* 8 (1), 123–8.

Greenhalgh, T. and Hurwitz, B. (1998) *Narrative-Based Medicine*. London: BMJ Books.

Grundy, S. (1987) *Curriculum: Product or Praxis*? New York. The Falmer Press.

Guba, E.G. and Lincoln, Y.S. (1981) *Effective Evaluation: Improving the Usefulness of Evaluation Results through Responsive and Naturalistic Approaches*. San Francisco: Jossey–Bass.

Guba, E. and Lincoln, Y. (1994) 'Competing paradigms in qualitative research', in N. Denzin and Y. Lincoln (eds), *Handbook of Qualitative Research*. London: Sage. pp. 105–17.

Haigh, N. (1998) *Teaching about Reflection and Ways of Being Reflective*. New Zealand, University of Waikato. www.auckland.ac.nz/cpd/HERDSA/HTML/Workshop/Haigh.HTM (accessed February 2006).

Handy, C. (1988) *Understanding Organisations*, 3rd edition. London: Penguin.

Hanley, B., Truesdale, A., King, A., Elbourne, D. and Chalmers, I. (2001) 'Involving consumers in designing, conducting and interpreting randomised controlled trials: questionnaire survey', *British Medical Journal,* 322: 519–23.

Haralambos, M. and Holborn, M. (1991) *Sociology: Themes and Perspectives*. London: Collins Educational.

Harré, R. (1972) *The Philosophies of Science*. Oxford: Oxford University Press.

Hart, C. (1998) *Doing a Literature Review: Releasing the Social Science Research Imagination*. London: Sage.

Hart, E. and Bond, M. (1996) *Action Research for Health and Social Care: A Guide to Practice*. Buckingham: Open University Press.

Hawkins, P. and Shohet, R. (2000) *Supervision in the Helping Professions*, 2nd edition. Buckingham: Open University Press. (1st edition 1989.)

Heron, J. (1996) *Co-operative Inquiry: Research into the Human Condition*. London: Sage.

Hollingsworth, S. (1994) *Teacher Research and Urban Literacy Education: Lessons in a Feminist Key*. New York: Teachers College, University of Columbia.

Hollingsworth, S. (ed.) (1997) *International Action Research: A Casebook for Educational Reform*. London: The Falmer Press.

Iles, V. and Sutherland, K. (2001) *Organisational Change*. London: NCCSDO.

Jarvis, P. (1999) *The Practitioner Researcher*. San Francisco: Jossey–Bass.

Katz, J. and Martin, B. (1997) 'What is research collaboration?', *Research Policy*, 26: 1–18.

Kemmis, S. (1982) *The Action Research Planner*. Geelong, Vic.: Deakin University Press.

Kemmis, S. and McTaggart, R. (2000) 'Participatory action research', in N. Denzin, and Y. Lincoln (eds), *Handbook of Qualitative Research*. 2nd editiion. Thousand Oaks, CA: Sage. pp. 567–606.

Kemmis, S. and Wilkinson, M. (1998) 'Participatory action research and the study of practice', in B. Atweh, S. Kemmis and P. Weeks (eds), *Action Research in Practice: Partnerships for Social Justice in Education*. London: Routledge. pp. 21–36.

Knowles, M. (1970) *The Modern Practice of Adult Education: Andagogy versus Pedagogy*. New York: Association Press.

Kolb, D. (1984) *Experiential Learning*. Englewood Cliffs, NJ: Prentice Hall.

Lewin, K. (1946) 'Action research and minority problems', *Journal of Social Issues*, 216 (2): 34–46.

Lewin, K. (1951) *Field Theory in Social Science*. New York: Harper & Row.

Lincoln, Y. and Guba, E. (1985) *Naturalistic Inquiry*. Newbury Park, CA: Sage.

Lincoln, Y. and Guba, E. (2003) 'Paradigmatic controversies – contradictions and emerging confluences', in N. Denzin and Y. Lincoln (eds), *The Landscape of Qualitative Research – Theories and Issues*. Thousand Oaks, CA: Sage.

Lomax, P., Evans, M. and Parker, Z. (1996) 'Working in partnership to enhance self-study within teacher education'. www.bath.ac.uk/~edsajw/lomax/draft1.htm (accessed February 2006).

McGinnis, J.R. (2001) 'The use of a practitioner research strategy, cases in a large-scale teacher enhancement project'. www.towson.edu/csme/mctp/research/AETS2001.htm (accessed February 2006).

McLeod, J. (1999) *Practitioner Research in Counselling*. London: Sage.

McLeod, J. (2003) *Doing Counselling Research,* 2nd edition. London: Sage.

McNiff, J. (2000) *Action Research in Organisations*. London: Routledge.

McNiff, J. (2002) *Action Research: Principles and Practice,* 2nd edition. London: Routledge Falmer. (1st edition, Routledge, 1992.)

McTaggart, R. (1994) 'Participatory action research: issues in theory and practice', *Educational Action Research*, 2 (3): 313–37.

Martin, P. (1999) 'Influences on clinical judgement in mental health nursing', *NT Research*, 4 (4): 273–81.

Maruyama, G. (1996) 'Application and transformation of action research in educational research and practice', *Systems Practice*, 9 (1): 85–101.

Maturana, H. and Varela, F. (1980) *Autopoiesis and Cognition: The Realization of the Living*. Dordrecht: D. Reidel.

Matthews, J. (2003) 'A framework for the creation of practitioner-based evidence', *Education and Child Psychology*, 20 (4): 60–7.

Maxwell, J. (1992) 'Understanding and validity in qualitative research', *Harvard Educational Review*, 62: 279–300.

Mezirow, J. (1991) *Transformative Dimensions of Adult Education*. San Francisco: Jossey–Bass.

Morgan, D. (1998) 'Practical strategies for combining qualitative and quantitative methods: applications to health research', *Qualitative Health Research*, 8 (3): 362–76.

Morse, J. (ed.) (1991) *Qualitative Nursing Research – A Contemporary Dialogue*. Newbury: Park, CA: Sage.

Morse, J., Barrett, M., Mayan, M., Olson, K. and Spiers, J. (2002) 'Verification strategies for establishing reliability and validity in qualitative research', *International Journal of Qualitative Methods*, 1 (2): 1–19.

NMC (Nursing and Midwifery Council) (2004) 'The Nursing and Midwifery Code of Professional Conduct: Standards for Conduct, Performance and Ethics'. www.nmc-uk.org (accessed February 2006).

Pawson, R. and Tilley, N. (1997) *Realist Evaluation*. London: Sage.

Popper, K. (1959) *The Logic of Scientific Discovery*. London: Hutchinson.

Rearick, M. and Feldman, A. (1999) 'Orientations, purposes and reflection: a framework for understanding action research', *Teaching and Teacher Education,* 15: 333–49.

Redfern, M., Keeling, S. and Powell, E. (2000) The Royal Liverpool Children's Inquiry, http://www.ncl inquiry.org.uk/index.htm published by the Stationary Office (accessed February 2006).

Richards, J. (1996) 'Turning to the artistic: developing an enlightened eye to creating teaching self-portraits'. www.educ.queensu.ca/~ar/sstep1996/janet.htm (accessed February 2006).

Richardson, S., Hastorf, A. and Dornbusch, S. (1964) 'Effects of physical disability on a child's description of himself', *Child Development,* 35: 893–907.

Robinson, V. (1993) *Problem-Based Methodology: Research for the Improvement of Practice*. Oxford: Pergamon Press.

Robson, C. (2002) *Real World Research*, 2nd edition. Oxford: Blackwell.

Sackett, D. and Wennberg, J. (1997) 'Choosing the best research design for each question', *British Medical Journal*, 315: 1636.

Schandt, T. (1994) 'Constructivist, interpretivist approaches to human inquiry', in N. Denzin, and Y. Lincoln (eds), *Handbook of Qualitative Research*. London: Sage.

Schon, D. (1983) *The Reflective Practitioner*. New York: Basic Books.

Schon, D. (1987) *Educating the Reflective Practitioner*. San Francisco: Jossey–Bass.

Senge, P. (1990) *The Fifth Discipline*. London: Century Business.

Shaw, I. (2002) 'Practitioner research: evidence or critique'. www.intsoceval.org/files/newyork/shaw.rtf (accessed February 2006).

Shulman, J.H. (2002) 'Happy accidents: cases as opportunities for teacher learning'. www.wested.org.online_pubs/happyaccidents.pdf (accessed February 2006).

Smith, D. and Katz, J. (2000) *Collaborative Approaches to Research*. London: Higher Education Funding Council England (HEFCE).

Smith, J. (ed) (2003) *Qualitative Psychology: A Practical Guide to Research Methods*. London: Sage.

Stiles, W. (1999) 'Evaluating qualitative research', *Evidence Based Mental Health*, 2 (4): 99–101.

Tesch, R. (1990) *Qualitative Research: Analysis Types and Software Tools*. New York: Falmer.

Thompson, C. and Dowding, D. (eds) (2002) *Clinical Decision Making and Judgment in Nursing*. Edinburgh: Churchill Livingstone.

Turner, M. and Beresford, P. (2004). *User Controlled Research: Its Meanings and Potential. Shaping Our Lives and the Centre for Citizen Participation*. Brunel University.

UNICEF (1990) 'Convention on the Rights of the Child.' Adopted and opened for signature, ratification and accession by General Assembly resolution 44/25 of 20 November 1989. Entry into force 2 September 1990, in accordance with Article 49.

Wade, D.T. (2005) 'Ethics, audit and research: all shades of grey', *British Medical Journal,* 330: 468–71.

Walker, J., Holloway, I. and Wheeler, S. (2005) 'Guidelines for ethical review of qualitative research', *Research Ethics Review,* 1 (3): 90–6.

Watzlawick, P. (1978) *The Language of Change*. New York: Basic Books.

Weiss, C.H. (1986) 'The many meanings of research utilisation', in M. Bulmer (ed.), *Social Science and Social Policy*. London: Allen & Unwin.

Whorf, B.L. (1956) *Language, Thought and Reality* (edited with an introduction by J. Carroll). New York: Wiley.

Index

Indexed by Caroline Eley.